God Is a
Black Woman

God Is a Black Woman

Christena Cleveland, PhD

HarperOne
An Imprint of HarperCollinsPublishers

The events and experiences detailed herein are all true and have been faithfully rendered as I have remembered them, to the best of my ability. Some names and identifying details have been changed to protect the privacy of the individuals involved.

Though conversations come from my keen recollection of them, they are not written to represent word-for-word documentation; rather, I've retold them in a way that evokes the real feeling and meaning of what was said, in keeping with the mood and spirit of the event.

HarperCollins books may be purchased for educational, business, or sales promotional use. For information, please email the Special Markets Department at SPsales@harpercollins.com.

FIRST EDITION

Designed by Dovetail Publishing Services

Library of Congress Cataloging-in-Publication Data available upon request.

ISBN 978-0-06-298878-2

22 23 24 25 26 LSC 10 9 8 7 6 5 4 3 2 1

for Des

"If the concept of God has any validity or any use,
it can only be to make us larger, freer, and more loving.
If God cannot do this, then it is time we got rid of Him."

— James Baldwin, *The Fire Next Time* —

"Gods die. And when they truly die they are unmourned
and unremembered. Ideas are more difficult to kill than
people, but they can be killed, in the end."

— Neil Gaiman, *American Gods* —

"The white fathers told us: I think, therefore I am.
The Black Mother within each of us—the poet—
whispers in our dreams: I feel, therefore I can be free."

— Audre Lorde, *Sister Outsider* —

contents

1

She Who Is Worth Seeking at All Costs

The terror exploded in my gut as soon as I heard the police sirens in the distance. They were coming for me.

Just moments earlier, I had crossed the cobblestone square in the quaint town of Mauriac, France, and entered its fortresslike basilica. As I examined the cavernous interior, I was aggressively confronted with signs forbidding visitors from trespassing beyond the crimson velvet ropes surrounding the town's renowned sixth-century statue of the Black Madonna, an uncommon dark-skinned version of the Virgin Mary. Even with my flailing grasp of the French language, I understood that if I disregarded the signs, I risked setting off the church's alarm system. But the ropes hung more than forty feet from the magnificent unapologetically-Black-and-female Madonna.

My unapologetically Black-and-female body longed to be near this Black Madonna, whom people of diverse races, religions, and eras have recognized as a Black and female image of God. Though I was raised in a Black family and had spent significant time in Black church spaces, the image of a white male God permeated my being. I know I am not alone. The late Black tennis star Arthur Ashe shared his childhood experience with white male God with a reporter from *Sports Illustrated,* who wrote: "Every Sunday, Arthur Jr. had to go to church, either First Presbyterian or Westwood Baptist, where his parents had met and where he would look up at a picture of Christ with blond hair and blue eyes and wonder if God was on his side."[1]

Like Arthur Jr., I too questioned whether God was on my side. And after years of questioning, healing, and transformation, I had traveled all the way to the heart of central France to finally come face-to-face with the Black Madonna. Desperate for a divine image that I related to and breathed hope into my experience as a Black person and as a woman, I had to be near this likeness of God that looked like me. Seeing Her from a roped off distance wasn't enough. I longed to gaze into Her mysterious and kind eyes, to witness Her unyielding clutch on Her precious Black boy, to run my fingers along Her centuries-old dark, wooden body, and to stand before a sacred image of Black femininity.

Eyeing the security cameras conspicuously aimed at the altar, I assessed the risks. On the one hand, I knew from experience that Black people and women are especially punished when we disregard rules. On the other hand, I knew that Black people and women are especially punished whenever we do pretty much anything. We live in a world that punishes us—for having opinions, for existing, for taking up space. As I stood at the edge of the Black Madonna of Mauriac's altar, I recalled the numerous beatings I had endured as a Black woman, much like this one:

I can't tell if you're sloppy or mischievous.

Those were the words a male audience member publicly said to me at the end of my academic lecture at Cambridge University. Drawing on my expertise as a social psychologist and theologian, I had just exposed the rampant racism in a famous Cambridge scholar's work and the scholar's fanboys were all up in arms. (I mean, *how dare I* critique their precious intellectual idol?) One fanboy attacked:

I can't tell if you're sloppy or mischievous.

Rather than offering a legitimate critique of my lecture, he fired off a racial-gender slur that cut to the core of my identity as Black and female. *Sloppy* is a delegitimizing stereotype launched at Black people. *Sloppy, dirty, lazy, worthless;* these are some of the labels society uses to brand us. And ever since good ol' Eve in the Garden of Eden, women have been saddled with the *mischievous* stereotype, especially when we disregard social norms and do unthinkable things like call out a scholar's racism. *Mischievous, deceptive, untrustworthy, morally weak;* these are the labels that society uses to bitch-slap us into submission.

I can't tell if you're sloppy or mischievous.

Right off the bat, as if it were already locked-and-loaded, his attack on my Blackness and femaleness was so precise, he might as well have said, *I can't tell if you're Black or female.*

I can't tell if you're sloppy or mischievous.

The memory of such beatings continued to clang in my soul as I stood in the basilica of Mauriac just forty feet away from an ancient statue of the divine Black and female One, who is neither sloppy, nor mischievous. There She stood, head held high, Black skin glimmering in the candlelight, Her fierce gaze a declaration to the whole world: "Go on, *I dare you* to call me sloppy or mischievous."

"Yeah," I murmured to myself. "No rope or threat of alarms is gonna stop me from getting near Her."

I removed my walking boots so as not to soil the carpeted altar and lifted my sock-covered foot to step over the rope barrier. As soon as my big toe crossed the vertical plane, a ferocious, ear-piercing, pew-rattling alarm sounded. Knowing I only had seconds before I was discovered, I made a mad dash across the length of the altar to kiss Her wooden feet and quickly look up to receive Her gaze, half expecting Her to shoot me an approving wink.

Harsh emergency lights illuminated the once-dark sanctuary as I ran back across the rope and scrambled to pull on my boots. By the time I reached the basilica door, I could hear the faint but familiar NEE-yoo-NEE-yoo-NEE-yoo-NEE-yoo sound of French police sirens coming for me. My heart rate quickened as I thrust open the heavy wooden-and-iron doors, stumbled into the ghost-townlike plaza, and frantically searched for a place to hide out. I could hear the sirens coming closer, but there was nowhere to go! In every direction, all I could see was a deserted cobblestone square, empty post-tourist season sidewalk cafes, and shuttered shops.

Terrified of being caught, arrested, and whoknowswhat, I ran along the edges of the plaza, looking for an open door.

As the sirens grew louder and a squad of police cars rounded the corner into the town square, I tripped on my still-untied shoelaces and tumbled into an empty restaurant covered in outdated, forest-green velour decor. Pulling myself up off the floor, I ignored the bartender's gaping stare and immediately sought refuge in the restroom.

Inside the tiny bathroom, I could hear police car doors slamming and police boots lumbering down the street in search of the person who had set off the basilica alarm. Despite my absolute terror, while hiding out in a European toilet room, I finally had a legitimate reason to ask myself a question I had been longing to ask, "What would Jason Bourne do?"

Knowing the answer to that question, I immediately attempted to disguise myself. First, I changed my hair by patting down my afro and putting on my black ski hat in order to cover my distinctive curls. Then I put on my large black sunglasses. Finally, I removed my bright red overcoat and stuffed it into my backpack, leaving me with just my thin black fleece and black pants. Examining myself in the cracked mirror, I surveyed my new look: black hat, black sunglasses, black fleece, black pants, Black skin.

"What are you doing?" I interrogated myself, side-eyeing my reflection in the mirror. "You. Are. Not. Jason. Bourne. It doesn't matter if you put on a hat. No matter how you try to disguise yourself, you'll still be a Black woman in rural France. You. Can't. Hide."

Feeling sheepish, I continued staring in the mirror. I could still hear the police looking for me, so I decided my best bet was to try to stay completely out of sight until the search was complete.

But when I exited the bathroom, the bartender pointed my ass toward the door. I suppose he wasn't in the mood to harbor a fugitive. So, looking left and right for the French po-po, I left the restaurant and began making my way around the town square searching for another open business in which to hide. Within moments, I realized that several police officers were still patrolling the area by squad car, so I jumped behind one of the massive stone pillars dotting the edge of the square. The pillars became my police shields as I laboriously hopped from one to the next, keeping one eye open for roaming cops and another eye peeled for the next place to hide. It was early in the afternoon, and most businesses in rural France close during the afternoon. I was getting desperate. I wasn't sure how long I could hold off these relentless police officers. Their intensity revealed the truth that many priceless Black Madonnas have been stolen. After unsuccessfully trying to enter a tea shop, a dress shop, a bookstore, and even a butcher, I eventually came upon an enchanting chocolate shop that was *OUVERT*!

I don't even eat chocolate. I gave up sugar years ago (more on that later) but that whimsical, straight-out-of-the-movie *Chocolat* shop might as well have been my own personal heaven. As I entered the warm, light-filled space and ran my fingers along the millennial pink subway tiles that covered the walls, I half-expected Juliette Binoche to pop out from behind the counter.

The actual owner, Martine, spoke a little bit of English and warmly welcomed me into her shop. With my heart still pounding and one ear extended toward the ongoing sirens, I explained to her that all of the police commotion was about me and that I needed a place to hide. With a gleam in her eye and an affirming nod, she silently offered me a corner table away from the window and set off to make me a pot of floral white tea.

Still on edge, I dropped my bag and sat perched on the chair, expecting the French police to violently burst into the beautiful and serene chocolate shop and drag me away in handcuffs any moment. As I awaited the worst, I realized that the terror in my bones was a familiar one. As a Black woman in a white male God's world, I had been a fugitive my entire life.

A Fugitive at Five

Much like little Arthur Jr., I first experienced the terror of white male God when I was just a munchkin. Immediately after I graduated from kindergarten, the summer of 1986, I spent almost every day in church. My resourceful mother had signed me up for every Vacation Bible School (VBS)—a weeklong "Sunday School"–type program hosted by white evangelical churches—in a twenty-mile radius. VBS was a cost-effective alternative to daycare, so each week she dropped me and my older brother and younger sister at yet another church where our Black bodies were engulfed by a sea of whiteness. A precocious child, I didn't love the soulless VBS songs and, though it wasn't until college that I encountered the academic term *theodicy*, I was already beginning to question how a "loving God" could possibly commit global genocide by flood (not the questions the leaders with cutesy, felt-board animals going two-by-two onto Noah's ark thought we'd be asking). But I endured VBS because my mom told me to go, and I prided myself on being an obedient child.

One week, as soon as our mom dropped us off at a VBS in Castro Valley, California, I gleefully spotted a towering tetherball set on the church's asphalt playground. I loved playing tetherball! We had a homemade tetherball set in our backyard complete with a bald tire-and-cement base, and just seeing the tetherball set at this unfamiliar church put me at ease.

"Look!" I said to my brother John-John, directing his attention to the tetherball across the blacktop. "We're going to have so much fun this week!"

At the first recess break, John-John and I sprinted to the tetherball and immediately got lost in a competitive game. We must have missed our teacher's call to return to the classroom because the next thing we heard was, "Get in here, you niggers!"

We both froze. The tetherball whizzed and spiraled around the pole.

As a five year old, I hadn't yet acquired this new vocab word, but I instinctively understood that it was negative and that it referred to me. I knew my brother and I looked different than our classmates and it didn't take long for me to deduce that *nigger* was about my Blackness and that it was bad. This rudimentary knowledge was enough to make me duck my head in terror-induced shame. As I ran toward the classroom, I knew in my little Black-girl body that I was not safe around this teacher. The terror began simmering in my bones.

At the time, I figured that this teacher's attack on my Black existence was an isolated incident in a world that is otherwise safe and loving toward little Black bodies. Back then, I didn't know that anti-Blackness exists in much more subtle forms, and that being called a nigger at VBS was simply the tip of the iceberg in white male God's chilly world. But as I grew older and encountered anti-Blackness in both its blatant and almost-undetectable forms, I began to notice the terror I first experienced at VBS rose from simmering to brewing. The terror eventually boiled over in 2016, the year that finally sent me thundering toward the Sacred Black Feminine.

In 2016, it wasn't just white VBS teachers calling Black kids *niggers*. That year, it seemed like every damn week we were collectively traumatized by the publicized killings of unarmed Black people by armed police. Like many other Black millennials, I responded to each lynching with the noblest resistance I could muster, while simultaneously trying to manage my own terror and PTSD from repeatedly seeing videos of Black people who look just like me being shot and killed by the police.

At the time, I was a columnist for *Christianity Today* (*CT*) magazine, a widely read national publication with such a predominantly white, politically conservative readership that my friends and I called it *Christianity Yesterday* magazine. In an attempt to awaken *CT*'s readers to the reality of anti-Black police brutality, I wrote a completely nonshocking essay about the historical inaccuracy of "white Jesus." As we know, scholars agree that despite the plethora of blond-haired, blue-eyed images of Jesus that poison our collective imagination, the actual historical Jesus basically looked like a modern-day Arab man. In my essay, I implored readers to recognize that if their own Christ had dark skin, then certainly they must stop tossing a callous and defensive "but All Lives Matter" retort in the general vicinity of Black people crying out for justice and, instead, do everything they can to ensure that Black lives do, in fact, matter.

Somehow, my completely nonshocking essay shocked the *CT* readers and sent them into a disintegrating spiral. Though I was accustomed to receiving a good amount of hate mail from *CT* readers, I wasn't prepared to receive eleven times as much hate mail as normal and four death threats. Since some of the threats were sent to my job and others were sent to my house, where I lived alone, I felt unsafe in both places. My hands quivered incessantly for weeks as my fear of this white male God and his minions brewed.

Is There Any Hope?

The day after the 2016 presidential election, I visited New Orleans, one of the most politically progressive cities in the South. While wandering the working art studios in the Bourbon Street area, I encountered a white sculptor who, upon hearing that I taught at Duke Divinity School, burst into zealous tears. Her collar soggy with snot and runny mascara, she articulated the disillusionment that many New Orleanians felt in the aftermath of Trump's election.

"This election is so devastating," she lamented. "Is there any hope? Where is God in the midst of this?"

Her sorrow didn't surprise me; after all, over 80 percent of New Orleans's voters had opted for Hillary Clinton. Moreover, I could easily connect the dots between her sense of abandonment in the political realm and her earnest questioning of God's reliability in the midst of her pain. Though all terror is painful, she wasn't just experiencing a finite terror like "this particular person or situation is unsafe." Rather, she was experiencing a comprehensive terror like "the world is completely unsafe, and I now know I cannot trust the people and institutions I've trusted in the past." This type of terror is incredibly destabilizing, and her spiritual belief system crumbled under its weight.

This election is so devastating. . . . Is there any hope? Where is God in the midst of this?

This is a question Black people have been collectively asking for centuries as we have been traumatized by one bogus elected official after another. It's a question that Black LGBTQ+ people have been asking as they encounter persistent condemnation and rejection in many Black church spaces. It's a question that more and more white women like the New Orleanian sculptor have been asking since Donald Trump was elected and Judge Brett Kavanaugh was appointed to the Supreme Court despite being accused of sexually assaulting Dr. Christine Blasey Ford, a white woman. It's a question many American citizens have asked of a government supposedly founded on "Christian" values, yet systematically terrorizes, imprisons, and divides the families of undocumented immigrants. It's a question that people are asking globally as the COVID-19 pandemic continues to collaborate with social inequality to ravage the most vulnerable. All over the world, the belief in a God who is *with* us and *for* us is cracking.

The question, *Is there any hope? Where is God in the midst of this?* reverberates in our souls and quickly rises to the surface during times of terror because spirituality, in part, is about relying on a Power greater than ourselves. During times of fear, uncertainty, and distress, many spiritual people look to the Divine for protection, clarity, and guidance. In fact, this behavior is modeled in the book of Psalms: "I look to the hills, where does my help come from? My help comes from the Lord." Especially when we feel our own power crumbling, spirituality offers a loving connection to a steadfast, reliable Power.

But what happens when you can't trust the Power you're supposed to rely on? What happens when that Power is so closely linked to human greed, political power, patriarchy, and white supremacy that it is no longer recognizable? What happens when that Power has been irrevocably corrupted? What happens when that Power is printed on the coins and bills, gets Donald Trump elected, ignores Black people's and women's testimonies, banishes LGBTQ+ people from church, and hoists All Lives Matter and Blue Lives Matter

signs in the wake of yet another police shooting of an unarmed Black person? Then where do you turn? In a world
full of hopelessness, is hope even worth seeking?

The Idea of God

Let's pull back for a minute to study the idea of God. If you
close your eyes and try to imagine God, what image comes
to mind? Even if we don't call ourselves spiritual or religious,
Gods matter because ideas matter. Ideas are deceptively powerful. Even when we barely pay them any conscious attention, ideas have the power to change our emotions, thoughts,
and behaviors. Take the idea *time flies*. Though *time flies* is a
commonly used figure of speech in North American culture,
it doesn't play an official role in our society. It's not written
on the wall at the post office, it isn't recited during religious
services, and it's not publicly debated. It's simply taken for
granted that "time flies." In other words, time runs out; it's
in short supply; it's a scarce commodity. But this simple idea
shapes North American culture in powerful ways. For example, the idea that *time flies* affects our emotions; for instance,
it's considered rude to arrive late to a meeting and we often
feel embarrassed when we do so. The idea that *time flies* also
affects our thinking; we tend to think of time in terms of its
monetary value. We even use phrases like "time is money"
and often think of time as an "investment." The idea that *time
flies* also affects our values and behaviors; we "spend time"
doing the things we value, whether it is earning money, caring for our loved ones, or bingeing on Netflix. Compared to

countries in the global south, where time is seen as abundant, Americans spend less time cultivating friendships and more time working. Similarly, family dinner time is a much briefer affair in the United States than in the global south.

Fellow social psychologist Hazel Markus teaches us that ideas shape culture more powerfully than anything else.[2] According to Markus, ideas shape culture by directly influencing the types of institutions, everyday practices, and individuals that exist within the culture. For example, the idea that *time flies* significantly shapes the institution of "family dinner" by shortening it. The idea that *time flies* significantly shapes our everyday practices by decreasing our time spent with friends. And the idea that *time flies* significantly shapes our individual experiences by triggering embarrassment when we are late. Yet we aren't often aware that we are so intensely shaped by the idea that *time flies*. Even if we regret not having more time with family and friends or wish we weren't always rushing from one meeting to the next, we rarely stop to consider that these behaviors are induced by the cultural idea that *time flies*. Rather, we blame ourselves for not being able to juggle a million balls at once. We don't pause to examine which ideas govern our culture and how they shape us. In this remarkably crafty way, ideas fly under the radar while powerfully impacting us.

If the idea that *time flies* has the power to shape my emotions, thoughts, and behaviors, then what about the idea of God?

I recently spoke on the topic of religion and culture at a university in the Pacific Northwest. Immediately after my lecture, a white student approached me and asked, "Does it make Black people uncomfortable that God is a white man?" Though I had made no direct reference to God's race or gender in my lecture, the student assumed that God is white and male. This student's question shines a glaring light on the idea of God as a white man that distinctly shapes our American culture. Everywhere we turn, there are pictures of God as a white male—in churches, films, and everyday conversation. The prevalence of white male images of God easily lead us to conclude that God is definitively and exclusively white and male. And like many culture-shaping ideas, we don't even question the idea or how it shapes our thoughts, emotions, and behaviors. For most of us, regardless of what we might *want* to believe or *claim* to believe, the image that immediately comes to mind when we imagine God is that of a powerful white man who is *for* and *with* powerful white men. It's a deceptive idea that flies under the radar, powerfully shaping us without our consent.

But if we examine this idea, we'll uncover its sinister origins and how those sinister origins echo today, shaping our culture in dehumanizing ways. We will begin to see that our idea of God determines who is sacred and who is profane, whose life matters and whose does not, whose testimony is believable and whose is not, who is a fugitive and who is not, and who is safe and who is not. And as we continue our exploration, we will begin to wonder if this white male God is on the side of *any* living beings. We will also discover that even though this white male God is the patron of mediocre white men—fueling their unmerited audacity to dominate this world—he infects all of us.

Hope Is Here

Being both Black and female in the aftermath of Trump's election in 2016, I was beginning to connect the dots between the cultural idea of a white male God and my incessant fear as a Black woman. There was just one problem. I had no idea where to turn. Imagination is theology; we can only believe what we can imagine. And our cultural landscape hasn't given us many tools to imagine a non-white, non-male God.

My whole life, I had been indoctrinated into American society's constrictive worship of a white male God; my spiritual imagination didn't know how to venture beyond the Protestant white male God that colonized and subdued America's spiritual imagination. As I came to learn, this is exactly where patriarchy wants us—without an adventurous spiritual imagination, without the audacity to ask boundary-pushing questions about God, and without a connection to our true, uncontrollable power. In order to encounter the divine truth that lies beyond what we think we know, we have to excavate our cultural landscape to uncover the hidden work of this white male God and forge a new path.

In early 2017, I mustered all of the desperate courage I could find and took one single, trembling step away from all I had known and all I had been taught to ask. With this step, I began anxiously searching for images of what I call the Sacred Black Feminine, a divine being who stands *with* and *for* Black women because She Herself is a Black woman. Thankfully, I didn't have to search far. Just beyond the Protestantism of my origins and from the mystical depths of rogue Catholicism, rose the Black Madonna, a Black female image of the divine who is often claimed by Catholicism but draws seekers of all religions and spiritualities.

Within seconds of viewing photos of Black Madonnas, my gut shifted from terror to hope. Before I even read a word about the Black Madonna, my *soul* immediately recognized that these photos and drawings of ancient Black Madonnas declared a truth about my own sacredness and gave birth to a new understanding of God.

I call Her the Sacred Black Feminine. She is the God who is *with* and *for* Black women because She *is* a Black woman. She is the God who definitively declares that Black women—who exist below Black men and white women at the bottom of the white male God's social pecking order—not only matter but are *sacred*. And, in doing so, She declares that *all* living beings are sacred. She is the God who smashes the white patriarchy and empowers us all to join in Her liberating work. She is the God who has a special love for the most marginalized because She too has known marginalization. She is the God who cherishes our humanity and welcomes our fears, vulnerabilities, and imperfections. Like a loving parent responding to a child's cry, She is the God who promises to come to our aid when we call out to Her, no questions asked. She is the God in whom we *can* find hope.

The Black Madonna images depicting the fiercely kind Sacred Black Feminine showed me that my terror was not only valid but is echoed around the world across the racial, gender, religious, and class spectrums, and across time. Indeed, the Black Madonna is simply one manifestation of the interfaith Sacred Black Feminine. Within a matter of minutes, I went from a Black woman woefully unconscious of the Sacred Black Feminine to one deeply devoted to the Black Madonna and now connected to a global lineage of marginalized people who have found hope in Her. My devotion was not short-lived; over the following months, I devoured every book I could find on Her and the people who have loved Her. In my research, I learned that there are over 450 Black Madonnas around the world, most of whom are over a thousand years old, with names as illustrious as Our Lady of the Good Death, Slave Mama, and Dear Dark One. I also found my own story in the divine stories of the Black Madonnas who, as fellow Black women, could intimately relate to my experiences. I wanted to learn more—to experience more—about these Black Madonnas who were cracking me open and meeting me where I was. But I needed a final push from Old Katerin.

She Who Is Forged in the Fire

Theologian Clarissa Pinkola Estés tells a story about her grandmother Old Katerin, a socioeconomically oppressed, rural, immigrant woman of color who maintained several fires in order to cook her food, heat water for bathing, and keep the house warm. A devout Catholic and lover of the Black Madonna, Old Katerin ritually sifted through the ashes of the fires each night looking for any remnant of burnt wood that resembled the feminine form. Every once in a while, she would find one and would exclaim: "She came to us! She's here with us!"[3]

You see, Old Katerin was determined to find the Sacred Black Feminine in the ashes. Pinkola Estés writes, "Old Katerin said this Black Holy Mother carried wisdom and knowledge, and understanding about repairing the land and making things grow." Old Katerin understood that the Sacred Black Feminine not only exists in the ashes of life, She also has the power to heal us and make us grow despite white patriarchy's devastating impact on us.

Every so often the white male parish priest would drop by the house and derogate Old Katerin's growing collection of burnt Black Madonnas. Pinkola Estés writes, "He said she was having a mere 'superstition' and wanted her to realize the Virgin was actually golden-haired with ringlets, porcelain skin, and rich-colored silk clothing." But Old Katerin ignored the priest, insisting that God was powerfully present in her burnt, seemingly unimpressive Black Madonnas.

"Old Katerin used to say that this was the point about her Black Madonnas taken from the fire . . . and about us too: That the little dark Blessed Mother was burned, but she was not consumed. She is still here. We are still here. We still hold our holy shapes, no matter what fire we have been passed through. Black Madonna says, 'Behold my dark face, my burned body, and grow, grow, flourish, flourish. Let nothing hold you back.' Black Madonna, forged in the fire, leads the way."[4]

When I first heard this story, I was overcome with awe for badass Old Katerin who—despite her lack of money, formal education, or male identity—decried her priest's pejorative teaching and instead forged her own magical and faithful pathway to a divine being who stood with her and affirmed her. But my soul longed for more than book knowledge; I needed to come face-to-face with the Sacred Black Feminine. Old Katerin's relentless search for the Sacred Black Feminine inspired me to go on my own journey. So, in the fall of 2018, I embarked on a four-hundred-mile walking pilgrimage across the Auvergne, a mountainous region in central France that hosts over forty ancient Black Madonna statues. My desire to be transformed by the Sacred Black Feminine sent me walking all over a winter mountain range in order to visit eighteen Black Madonnas. My desire to be transformed by the Sacred Black Feminine sent me deep into the dark forests of my trauma, so I could be healed. My desire to be transformed by the Sacred Black Feminine sent me away from the harmful spiritual communities of my origins so I could find true Love. My desire to be transformed by the Sacred Black Feminine sent me defiantly across the forbidden altar rope in order to touch the Black Madonna of Mauriac.

Back in the chocolate shop, where I sat tucked away as a fugitive, I could still hear the sirens circling the town square in search of me. As I awaited the fall of darkness when I could stealthily make my way back to my lodging, I looked through the window toward the basilica. I could feel the Black Madonna's empowering, approving gaze and my adrenaline relaxed. Like Old Katerin's burnt Black Madonnas, the Black Madonna of Mauriac's Black female body assured me that She understood my Black female terror for She too had been burned. However, She had not been consumed. Like Old Katerin, I knew I could trust the Sacred Black Feminine to heal my Black female embodied soul. I knew I could trust Her as I continued on my journey toward growth and flourishing. As I took my final sips of tea, I relished these truths, for I knew that much of my journey still lay ahead. I knew that in order to truly heal, I would need to bravely examine my burns. I would need to take a deep dive into my past to examine the ways I had been consumed by the white male God's fire. I would need to uncover the painful truth about how the white male God terrorizes us all.

2

in god we *can't* trust:
the problem with whitemalegod

was only three years old when I met Des but I swear it was love at first sight. The moment my newborn sister Des came home from the hospital, I peered into her crib and instantly recognized her as my kindred-spirit-sister. Though her verbal communication was limited, her joyful cackle and sparkling black eyes wooed my heart. When Des and I were little, we shared a room that was so tiny we could only fit our two twin beds in the room if they lay side by side, kissing. I don't know why we even bothered to keep both beds; we usually slept in the same bed anyway.

Des never stopped singing and dancing, and her joy brought vibrant life to my studious, serious existence. Each morning, as we huddled over our home's only bathroom vanity, Des broke into a full Broadway routine, often grabbing whatever was available—a jump rope, our mom's hot comb, my toothbrush—as a microphone. Before long, she crowded me out of the mirror. Des was simply a star and there was only room for one star in our little bathroom.

Each week at church, Des was assigned a Bible verse to memorize. But Des understood the world through music; naked words confounded her. So, each week after church as we walked around the lake in our California town, our family collaboratively put Des's verse to song so that Des could then sing it to herself all week. As we walked under the clear moonlight and past the Canadian geese that populated the lake, Des and I held hands, sometimes temporarily separated by Des's bippity-boppity movement but forever bonded by kindred-spirit-sisterhood. On those walks, I dreamt of Des starring in a Broadway musical. It was her destiny.

I was a psychology graduate student living in Santa Barbara when Des stopped dancing and singing and began to descend into a murky cloud of mental decay, suicidal ideation, and seizures. Her mental illness became so impossible to manage that she had to drop out of college. Though I wasn't particularly knowledgeable about clinical psychology, I knew enough to recognize that Des's psychotic spiral had biological underpinnings. I told her that she had a real illness and repeatedly encouraged her to seek professional help. One day, she called me from one of the restroom stalls at her job as a receptionist at a for-profit technical school.

Her cries pierced my heart as she maniacally screamed into the phone, "God wants me dead! God hates me! God is going to kill me!" I could hear her banging her forehead and crashing her body into the metal partitions encapsulating the stall. I later learned that her supervisor was so concerned that he called 911, and when the first responders subdued Des and carried her out of the building, the onlooking students mocked her, calling her the "crazy Black lady."

Imagine the terror of slowly losing your grip on reality and not knowing what is happening to you and being mocked by the people in your community. Where is God then?

Though no longer the case today, back then our earnest Black parents were ignorant of the realities of mental illness. Shaped by their devout belief in a white male God who only deals in the spiritual realm, they assumed that Des's illness was essentially a spiritual problem and encouraged Des to "praise God more." Not surprisingly, the racially diverse people in my parents' church parroted their advice and even distanced themselves from Des when she was exhibiting psychotic behaviors.

Imagine the terror of slowly losing your grip on reality and not knowing what is happening to you and being told by your parents and your spiritual community that you need to pull yourself together in order to receive God's touch? Where is God then?

in god we *can't* trust

A few years after Des's first psychotic break, I took on the role of official caregiver, inviting Des to live with me after she was released from a fifteen-month stint in a mental-health residential program. At the time, I didn't know what I was signing up for; my education as a caregiver to someone who lives with debilitating mental illness was a baptism by fire. Des, who had been diagnosed with a constellation of mental illnesses ranging from schizophrenia to bipolar to major depression, needed hands-on help with bathing, eating, running errands, and managing her psychotic emotions. Des was completely overwhelmed by life. And I was completely overwhelmed as her sister and caregiver.

Each morning, before I commuted to my demanding job as a first-year, tenure-track psychology professor, I helped Des get up and wash, cooked her breakfast, and assisted her as she ate. I needed to make sure she consumed enough calories in the morning before I left because I couldn't be certain she would eat while I was gone all day. In the evenings, after I returned from work, I cleaned up any messes Des had made in my absence and tried to calm her heaving body and soothe her cries of terror, which often lasted deep into the night.

"God, don't kill me! God, don't hurt me! God, have mercy on me!" she shrieked again and again and again.

As I held vigil with her in our shared bedroom, I reminisced about young Des, who had been so vivacious, independent, and clear-headed before her first psychotic break at around age twenty. Bearing witness to her current state, I wept alongside her. Sometimes I sent out desperate prayers to the same god who terrified my sister, but the prayers seemed to ricochet off the walls and return to me empty.

In theory, God was supposed to be near. Christians call God *Immanuel* which means *God with us*. That is what I had grown up hearing at church, especially during the Christmas holiday season. We were told that there is a God who cares about us so much that he came to Earth as a human being to be with us on our turf and on our terms and relate to us as a fellow human.

"God is with me." I dutifully repeated aloud to myself in an attempt to disentangle the knot of fear and abandonment that had formed in my gut earlier. But the knot persisted. Despite how God had been described to me and what I was *supposed* to believe, I'd never felt more alone. I wanted desperately to believe I wasn't alone—that this God cared about my distress and my sister's health—but I couldn't because the god I experienced did not match up with the theory. The god I experienced in my Black female body was the god I had inherited from American society and from my parents. This god is the one we see on TV and in stained-glass windows and at church camp; the god whose name is faithfully printed on every US bill and coin; the god on whose "Word" witnesses swear as they participate in our racist justice system; the god of the 81 percent of white evangelicals who elected Donald Trump despite his hateful words and actions toward women, people of color, Muslims, and disabled people; the god that champions the capitalistic economy that values profits over people and systemically killed the most marginalized during the COVID-19 pandemic.

This was the god I inherited from broader society and from the spiritual community of my origins. This is the god I was instructed to trust. But no matter how hard I tried to convince my mind that this god was with me, my Black female body told me that he was not. In fact, my Black female body told me to be afraid. "Be very, very afraid," she whispered in my gut.

fatherskygod

Research on religious and spiritual beliefs teaches us that when we believe in a solely male god, we also believe that he only deals with spiritual matters, not physical matters like mental illness.[1] For example, comparative religion scholar Andrew Harvey writes, "The [teachings] of the Father, the patriarchal [teachings], are essentially [teachings] of transcendence; techniques that offer an escape from heartbreak, from this 'illusion,' as they've termed it from this body, from nature, into some detached, serene, static peace of timelessness and freedom."[2] In other words, male god is *transcendent*; he isn't found in the mundane, physical world. He is *up there*, in the spiritual realm. In fact, in order to reach him, we must heal ourselves of our human maladies, find ways to escape from the heartbreak of this life (e.g., "praise God more"), and be presentable to a male god who is deeply detached from the human condition.

Additionally, scholars who have studied the patriarchal forces in Christianity, Buddhism, Islam, Judaism, and numerous Indigenous spiritualities have concluded that the perception of God as solely transcendent is a distinctly masculine idea that only thrives when we silence the more feminine idea of God's intimate presence in our lives. When the feminine is silenced and God is exclusively masculine, he becomes a detached, off-planet god that I call *fatherskygod*. When we need him most, fatherskygod isn't anywhere to be found.

But fatherskygod did not always exist, nor did he always dominate the spiritual landscape. For much of early human history, the sky served as God's warm, inviting abode—a divine place that remained intimately connected to the human experience. As theologian Matthew Fox writes, "For the premoderns and Indigenous peoples everywhere, the sky was alive. It harbored God the Father, among others [e.g., God the Mother], and was full of watchful eyes tending to human needs."[3] However, fatherskygod thundered onto the scene when the Indo-European "battle-axe cultures"[4] of northern Europe emerged during the Mesolithic period (15000–8000 BCE). The Indo-Europeans (think, *Vikings*) were aggressive warriors who stood in stark contrast to the peaceful nomadic cultures of the era. Not surprisingly, the Indo-Europeans' male deity reflected the culture's values. Indeed, according to researcher Merlin Stone, the "Indo-European male deity . . . was most often portrayed as a storm god, high on a mountain, blazing with the light of fire or lightning."[5] Rather than imminent, tender, and watchful, this male god who lived in the sky was ominous and threatening, much like the Indo-Europeans.

In 2400 BCE, when these Indo-Europeans invaded and colonized the global south, they brought fatherskygod with them, eventually decimating the region's vibrant, centuries-long devotion to God the Mother, and significantly shaping humans' understanding of the Judeo-Christian deity *Yahweh*.[6] Centuries later, fatherskygod was even further popularized in the Greek myths of Zeus and other male gods who lived in the sky. For example, Zeus devoured Metis (the goddess of feminine wisdom) in order to abort a son he feared would eventually overpower him. Additionally, Zeus's own father, Cronus, consumed seven of his children for the same reason.[7] The detached, off-planet fatherskygods of Greek mythology rarely concerned themselves with the needs of humans. If they turned their attention to humans at all, it was in order to dominate them. As Fox writes, to fatherskygod "humans are basically of no particular significance in the universe."[8] Between the Indo-Europeans and Greek mythology, the idea of a fatherskygod who prefers violent power plays to caring for our human needs flourished.

Despite fatherskygod's ongoing and powerful presence in our contemporary society, we have all been exposed to a strong cultural belief that God exists, is with us, and is trustworthy. Regardless of whether we have spent time in formal religious settings or not, every time we look at a US coin or dollar bill, we're reminded that it is "in God we trust." During the Christmas season, we're taught about "Immanuel" coming as a babe in a manger to be God with Us. We're supposed to believe that God is on our side, that we don't need to be afraid, that our lives matter, that our bodies matter. But we feel it in our bodies and in our emotional experiences: we are not safe. This god is not with us. When all hope seems lost, when we are afraid, when we are confused, the god on the money cannot be trusted. In god we *can't* trust.

The pervasive idea of fatherskygod prevents us from imagining a God who is with us in the nitty-gritty realities of human life, a God who is with us in the restroom stall, walks with us as the onlookers deride us, embraces us when even the love of the people who claim to love us can't stretch to meet us where we are. Due to fatherskygod, we are unable to imagine a God who will meet us at the intersection of our limited understanding of mental illness and a loved one's psychotic break. We are unable to imagine a God who is with us while we wonder if our beloved sister will survive the night. We are unable to imagine a God who proclaims #blacklivesmatter, a God who says #metoo, a God who stands not atop the social hierarchy, but at the bottom with the people who have been cast aside, silenced, and forgotten. When god is solely male, he can only show up as fatherskygod who is nowhere near us.

However, when God is female or distinctly feminine, we see a different story. Harvey's research also revealed that "the Mother's [teaching] comes down from transcendence into immanence, down from the safety of detachment into the misery and glory of love."[9] Indeed, though many of us often conceive of Christ as solely male, the Divine Mother is the one who most closely represents the earthy, gritty, nearness of Jesus Christ who said, "Take, eat, this is my body. This is my blood." Because Christianity has been dominated by men, many of us make an easy connection between Christ and God the Father. But we rarely envision the Divine Mother who is evident in Christ. Specifically, we have a difficult time recognizing Christ's mothering behaviors and feminine characteristics. But Christian mystics throughout the centuries have savored the feminine in Christ and have affirmed it as the Divine Mother working within the person of Jesus Christ.

In the fourteenth century, Julian of Norwich invited us into her famous revelation of love when she wrote, "Jesus Christ . . . is our true Mother. We received our 'Being' from Him and this is where His Maternity starts."[10] But even earlier, thirteenth-century French nun Marguerite of Oingt spoke ecstatically of Christ's mothering: "Are you not my mother and more than my mother? The mother who bore me labored in delivering me for one day or one night, but You, my sweet and lovely Lord, labored for me for more than thirty years."[11] And in the twelfth-century, St. Bernard de Clairvaux made a most magical and graphic invitation into the Divine Mothering of Christ when he wrote, "Suck not so much the wounds as the breasts of the Crucified."[12] To these mystics, Jesus Christ possessed both masculine and feminine characteristics, and embodied both God the Mother and God the Father. Twentieth-century Pope John Paul I agrees; in 1978, he declared, "God is Father, but especially, Mother."[13] Together, these mystics invite those of us who are wary of Christianity's male dominance to join them in receiving Christ's mothering balm.

Indeed, the idea of God as Divine Mother is an imminent salve, for mothers are the ones who are *with us* in the messiness of life. Mothers and birth parents of all genders don't shy away from poopy diapers; they endure the dizzying fatigue of late-night feedings in order to nourish us; and they hold vigil when we are stricken with chicken pox. They are immanent, *especially* when we are a mess. They come running to our aid when we are sick, when we are bleeding, when we are puking, when we have diarrhea. Rather than telling us that we need to clean ourselves up, or start acting right, or fix ourselves, they love us as we are, taking great pride in their mothering role when we need them most.

So, if mothers are really incredible at being present in our pain, illness, weakness, need, and disillusionment, why don't we typically perceive God as Mother? Why doesn't our society's idea of God include mothering and femininity?

the toxic masculinity of god

I first noticed Christianity's distrust of feminine wisdom years ago when I began preaching every six weeks or so at the church I attended. Though some Christian congregations don't allow women to preach, this one not only allowed it but affirmed it. Nonetheless, each time I preached, a handful of white men would charge toward me immediately after the service and critique my sermon. Let me be clear: I'm an academic; I can recognize constructive feedback and am accustomed to receiving it. These men's critiques weren't constructive feedback; they were designed to cut me down to size. Over the several years that I regularly preached, I was repeatedly accused of being heretical, deceived, and a sheep in wolf's clothing. Though they attended a church that encouraged women to preach, these men were suspicious of feminine wisdom and had no qualms about communicating their distrust of my spiritual leadership. According to them, since God is male, men should possess all the spiritual authority. In a way, I didn't trust my own feminine wisdom because I put up with this misogyny for several years.

But one day, while preparing for a sermon, I stumbled across an astonishing revelation. In the Judeo-Christian Creation story, the serpent is depicted as a cunning force that lures Adam and Eve away from God. The serpent is understood to be the anti-God, the anti-Truth, the embodiment of deception. This I knew. What I didn't know is that the Hebrew people who first heard this story were shaped by the idea that the serpent was the symbol of feminine wisdom. Just like anyone in contemporary American culture would look at a swoosh and recognize it as a symbol of Nike, anyone in the ancient world would have immediately associated the serpent with feminine wisdom.

Indeed, archeologists have discovered figurines dating approximately 1200 BCE in the region that was Canaan during the time of the Hebrews.[14] These figurines depict the serpent as feminine wisdom and/or the divine feminine. The *serpent as feminine wisdom* was the broadly held cultural idea. So, when the male leaders retold the Creation story, their choice to position the serpent (of *all* of the animals in the Garden of Eden) as the embodiment of deception was a direct attack on feminine wisdom.

As Torah scholar Ivy Helman explains, the early Hebrew leaders wanted to distance their spirituality from the paganism that abounded in their region. Since many of the so-called pagans worshipped female deities, the Hebrew leaders hastily rejected the possibility that the Judeo-Christian God could also be female or have feminine qualities. Additionally, patriarchy—a social system in which men hold power and non-male people are generally excluded from it—played a role in silencing divine feminine wisdom. In a society marked by gender hierarchy, it simply wouldn't do for God to be female or have feminine characteristics. It also wouldn't do for women to believe they had access to truth that was supposedly reserved for men. So, in their retelling of the Creation story, the patriarchal Hebrew leaders led an assault on feminine wisdom by positioning the serpent as the anti-Truth—forging the idea that divine feminine wisdom, like the serpent, is to be mistrusted and rejected. The cultural idea of *male god* bulldozes over scripture that clearly depicts God as a spirit who possesses both masculine and feminine characteristics. And due to how Christianity and Judaism dominate the global culture, it's not hard to see why male god rules almost everywhere.

Male god is a patriarchal myth that attempts to declare that men are more sacred than women, non-binary, and gender-expansive people. Since male god was created to silence and control nonmen, male god's primary allegiance is with men and toxic masculinity. Though masculinity is intrinsically beautiful, it is designed to be in interdependent relationship with femininity. Characteristics that are often associated with masculinity—like assertiveness, independence, and agency—are healthiest when they are in partnership with characteristics that are often associated with femininity—like emotional expressiveness, interdependence, and nurturing.[15] Like yin and yang, masculinity only works when it is influenced by femininity. Fox said it well when he wrote, "The feminine is what holds the masculine in life."[16] When masculinity rejects feminine wisdom, it becomes a toxic caricature of itself. As a result, we are left with a *male god* that is not only masculine, but masculine in a way that crushes femininity. We are left with a *male god* that is not at all influenced by femininity. Rather, like the patriarchal Hebrew leaders of old, *male god* is threatened by femininity; it distances itself from femininity and rewards thoughts, emotions, and behaviors that are fueled by toxic masculinity.

For centuries, toxic masculinity has colonized our understanding of God by exterminating the voices of divine femininity. For example, when the fourth-century Catholic bishop arrived in Le-Puy-en-Velay, France, he was so threatened by the Indigenous peoples' worship of Cybele, an ancient dark goddess, that he destroyed the existing temple and built a cathedral atop its ruins. Rather than peacefully coexisting with the people who worshipped a dark divine feminine, the bishop violently gentrified their temple and annihilated their religion. Such a hostile, petulant, insecure act reveals a religious system deeply afraid of feminine power.

Male god is the bro god—the god that hears a US presidential candidate brag about sexual assault and dismisses it as "locker room talk." The god that presides over the Catholic church's and Buddhist Shambhala community's colossal cover-ups of sexual abuse. The god who systematically devalues "essential workers" such as childcare providers, urban teachers, and supermarket clerks, and then requires them to risk their lives to save the people who are privileged enough to work from home during a global pandemic. The god who ignores the glaring evidence that poverty is sexist, that simply being non-male puts one at staggeringly high risk of economic oppression. The god of the glass ceiling and the all-male boardroom table who is disinterested in the plight of working women.

However, the toxic masculinity of male god doesn't just silence women. It also silences every other gender identity. Since toxic masculinity cannot affirm femaleness, it definitely cannot affirm trans and non-binary gender identities. One way that toxic masculinity stifles such identities is by keeping society trapped in a gender binary that only acknowledges cisgender men and cisgender women. As a result, we often struggle to recognize that other possibilities exist. Even more, the gender binary impoverishes our spiritual imaginations, making it difficult for us to see that God exists within trans and non-binary experiences of gender.

As a cisgender woman, I wrestled with this reality as I wrote this book. I often wondered whether asserting that God is female and feminine further tethers us to a gender binary that excludes trans and non-binary people and insists that femininity is the only legitimate expression of femaleness. But as I have explored the roots of misogyny, I have come to believe that proclaiming God's femaleness and femininity is a crucial step on our collective journey toward liberation from toxic masculinity. As we will see throughout this book, femaleness is under constant attack and our sacred connection to femininity has been violently severed. If we bypass these significant wounds, society as a whole will never heal from misogyny, much less gender binaries. Though my book offers a creative exploration of God's femaleness and femininity, I hope that it will join with other creative explorations of *all* of God's genders and gender expressions.

In addition to silencing female, trans, and non-binary gender identities, male god fuels our cultural idea that God is transcendent. Remember fatherskygod? Male god who is rife with toxic masculinity and sits atop the social hierarchy is our contemporary capitalistic society's version of father-skygod. Male god only associates with people who move in his circles, have access to his club, and speak his language. He's the god who is up there, over there, across the way, out of reach. If we put on our Sunday best, pull ourselves up by our bootstraps, contort ourselves into someone we are not, reach high enough and hard enough, or scale the social ladder, we may be able to rub shoulders with him.

But he *never* stoops down to us. You don't see the Fortune 500 CEO hanging out with the undocumented immigrants who clean the corporate headquarters at night, do you?

slavery's white christ

But our cultural idea of God isn't just about his maleness. It's also about his whiteness; the way that white people, their customs, and beliefs are considered the gold standard by which all other people are negatively compared.[17] But God is not white. Obviously. So, how the hell did we end up with a white god who looks like Thor?

Since Christianity is the loudest, brashest, and most amplified spiritual force on the planet, it affects all of us, whether we identify as Christian or not. In Christianity, the most prominent idea of God is in the person of Jesus Christ, a Palestinian man of African descent. In fact, most scholars agree that the historical Jesus looked like a modern-day Arab.[18] Not surprisingly, the earliest known image of Jesus is a lovely 235 CE Egyptian Coptic fresco that depicts Jesus as a Black man surrounded by Black and brown people.

Despite this compelling historical evidence, *white christ*— the patron of white supremacy—became a global figure in 1526 as the cornerstone of the European and American colonial slave trade.[19] Though many of the images of white male Christ seem benign and even genteel, their origin and ongoing meaning are killing us. All ideas, even inaccurate ones, have immense power and the idea of white christ is no exception.

As historian and theologian Kelly Brown Douglas teaches us, the idea that race is hierarchical empowered slave-holding whites to capture and own people, while also empowering nonslaveholding whites to benefit from a racial caste system that granted poor whites liberties that were withheld from Blacks. In this way, all white people, rich or poor, benefited from the enslavement of Africans.

However, these white people encountered a moral dilemma. How could they participate in the inhumane business of slavery when the historical Christ basically looked just like the enslaved people? And how could they worship a Christ whose ministry and teachings clearly showed that he identified with and preferred the poor and oppressed? Additionally, whites had to deal with a practical dilemma. If the enslaved African people became aware of the true identity and the liberating teachings of Jesus, would they rise up and rebel?

So white people invented the *white christ*. One of white supremacy's most powerful myths, the idea of the *white christ* solved white people's moral and practical dilemmas. According to Douglas, the *white christ* essentially made slavery A-okay because, if Christ was white, then it was cool for white people to enslave non-white people and benefit from the enslavement of non-white people.[20] But the *white christ* didn't simply justify slavery; it also made a statement about who God is and what God cares about. Since the *white christ* more closely resembled whites than Blacks, God was obviously more concerned with the experiences and troubles of white people than the experiences and troubles of Blacks. Further, since the *white christ* identified with whites, God obviously preferred whites over Blacks. The *white christ* offered proof that God wasn't concerned with the plight of the oppressed. In other words, God was just fine with slavery and other forms of oppression. In this way, God was not only associated with whiteness, but specifically with white supremacy. In the *white christ*, God specifically chose white people over Black people.

The fiction of the *white christ* involved blatantly ignoring Jesus's liberating teachings or willfully misinterpreting them. In a sermon, one proslavery minister made this argument for slavery:

> Our Lord repeatedly spoke of slaves, especially in several of his parables, without the slightest intimation that he condemned slavery, and in such a way as plainly showed that he considered it lawful . . . We

are told, Matthew 8:23–35, that a Centurion came to Jesus beseeching him to heal his sick servant . . . If the holding of slaves had been sinful, Jesus would, we doubt not, have so informed [the Centurion].[21]

Though the historical Christ was a revolutionary known for his love for the oppressed, the idea of the *white christ* cunningly trumped historical fact and biblical accuracy in order to support white supremacy and align with the powerful white slaveholding and slavetrading men who ruled the global society.

As we know, ideas shape behaviors. Not surprisingly, the idea of the *white christ* fueled white people's abuse toward Black people. If God didn't care about, affirm, or protect the humanity of Black people, then why should whites? In fact, the more a white person was exposed to the cultural idea of the *white christ*, the more despicably they treated Blacks. While describing the religion of the *white christ*, Frederick Douglass asserted, "For all slaveholders with whom I have ever met, religious slaveholders are the worst . . . The religion of the south is a mere covering for the most horrid crimes—a justifier of the most appalling barbarity—a sanctifier of the most hateful frauds—and a dark shelter under which the darkest, foulest, grossest, and most infernal deeds of slaveholders find the strongest protection."[22]

Given how ideas shape our culture, it didn't take long for the idea of the *white christ* to infect our cultural beliefs and values. Since God was on the side of the white slaveholders and slavetraders and not at all concerned with the liberation of the enslaved Black people, people began to believe that God most closely identified with and valued the most powerful white men in society. And if God most closely identified with and valued the powerful white men, then God must be a powerful white man too.

For God so loved the powerful white men . . . because he was one of them.

Everyone else—white women, enslaved Black people, nonslaveholding whites, and Indigenous people—fell outside of God's holy huddle and were thus excluded from God's protection.

whitemalegod

A century and a half after Abraham Lincoln's Emancipation Declaration, the *white christ* is still alive and well, collaborating with *male god* to breathe white patriarchy into our spiritual imaginations. In a society that still values the cultures, experiences, and lives of whites more than Blacks, and men more than women, *whitemalegod* continues to justify the silencing, exclusion, and oppression of Black, Indigenous, and people of color—specifically, Black women, trans and non-binary people.

If the God that adorns the stained-glass windows of our chapels is a white man, then why should the congregants affirm and defend the humanity of Black women? If the God that is depicted in the sorrowful country western song is definitively white, then how are the listeners invited to empathize with Black pain? If God is white, then why should white feminism care about anything other than the plight of white women? If God is a powerful white man sitting atop the social hierarchy, then why should anyone care about Black transgender women, who languish at the bottom of the hierarchy? If God is a white man, then why shouldn't all non-whites and non-male people be forced to contort themselves into the tiny, toxic boxes that white patriarchy deems acceptable? If God's name is written right next to President George Washington—a powerful, white, slaveholding male—on the US dollar bill, then why should American voters elect anyone other than Donald Trump? Or, for that matter, Joe Biden?

Indeed, the god of America is a whitemalegod whose identity lies at the fatal intersection of white supremacy and toxic masculinity. The patron of white patriarchy, whitemalegod is designed to dwell among, identify with, and protect the power of white people and cisgender men. However, people of color, women, trans, and non-binary people who have been conditioned to believe in whitemalegod find ourselves wondering where God is as we face ongoing humiliation, dehumanization, oppression, and disillusionment. Whitemalegod is nowhere to be found because he was never designed to be with us, among us, or on our side. Rather than *God with Us,* he is *God* Not *with Us.*

But this truth is not evident to the many white people and cisgender men who live in persistent ignorance of the ways that whitemalegod protects their power in spiritual spaces and in broader society. To willfully awaken to awareness would require repentance and reparations, so many

white people and cisgender men of all races remain asleep
. . . and complicit. In fact, whitemalegod banks on their
complicity. For, as we'll see throughout this book (especially
in chapters 10 and 11), the intentional and unintentional
actions of white people and cisgender men powerfully fuel
and maintain whitemalegod's dominance.

Regardless of our racial and gender identities, the liberating Sacred Black Feminine personally invites each of us
to examine which god we have been implicitly taught to
worship and how that god has shaped us. A god who is exclusively white and male, or even predominantly white and
male, is *never* going to be safe because he cannot affirm the
sacredness of non-white and non-male people. Indeed, those
of us who do not conform to whitemalegod's exacting standards of whiteness and maleness are violently excluded from
all that is considered sacred. Nowhere is that more clear than
in the depictions of Black women throughout history.

wholly unholy

There's something very evil about the way Black women in
particular are perceived as distant from the Divine. It brings
to mind the Jezebel stereotype, the idea that Black women
are impure by nature—an idea which has long plagued Black
women. Sociologist David Pilgrim explains: "Historically,
white women, as a category, were portrayed as models of
self-respect, self-control, and modesty—even sexual purity,
but Black women were often portrayed as innately promiscuous, even predatory."[23] The Jezebel stereotype flourished

during slavery as justification for the consistent raping of Black female enslaved people. White men convinced themselves that Black women had insatiable appetites for sex. Therefore, they were always "asking for it."

But political scientist Melissa Harris-Perry believes that the Jezebel stereotype is much more insidious and lasting than most stereotypes. She teaches us, "Hypersexuality was more than a demeaning and false stereotype; this inaccurate portrayal was intentional. Myth advances specific economic, social, and political motives."[24] Theologian and psychologist Chanequa Walker-Barnes emphatically concurs, "The Jezebel stereotype was the first and most predominant image of Black womanhood in the United States precisely because it was critical to maintaining not only the American slave economy, but the ideology of White supremacy and Black inferiority as a whole."[25] Further, the Jezebel stereotype is one example of *misogynoir*, which is the hatred of Black women. More specific than misogyny, scholar Moya Bailey coined the term in order to distinguish the innumerable ways that Black women experience a racialized sexism that is distinct from the sexism that women of other races experience and distinct from the anti-Blackness that Black men experience.[26]

The Jezebel stereotype continues to thrive today, far outlasting the institution of American slavery. And just as Harris-Perry and Walker-Barnes assert, the Jezebel stereotype is an intentional myth that lives on after slavery precisely because it was never specifically about slavery or even sexual impurity. Rather, it was about the ongoing subjugation of and holistic inferiority of Black women. Indeed, in our contemporary society, the Jezebel myth has expanded; Black women are not only seen as sexually impure, but impure in every way. For example, a few years ago when I was still carrying the "racial reconciliation" banner, a white male pastor asked me for help. His mostly white church needed a music leader and he wanted to hire a person of color. I immediately thought of a Black woman I knew who'd potentially be a good fit. Since the pastor didn't know her, I offered to make an introduction. But the pastor rejected my offer and expressed his bias, "Ugh. No. She'll probably just sleep with everyone on the worship team." All he knew was that she was a Black woman and yet this seemed to be all he needed to know to determine that she was unfit to be a leader at his church. Clearly, the Jezebel myth lives on—not by merely labeling Black women as sexually impure, but by labeling them as wholly unholy and inherently unfit for spiritual leadership. According to our cultural conditioning, femininity is untrustworthy and Blackness is dirty. So Black femininity is perceived as wholly unholy—as far from God as possible.

Indeed, Blackness aside, it took years of reverse conditioning for me to start to get comfortable with the idea of a *feminine* God. In 2010, when I was twenty-nine years old, I participated in a four-week gender and spirituality seminar in Seattle. There, I was first meaningfully exposed to feminist ideas that questioned God's maleness and offered evidence of God's femaleness. These perspectives were water to my soul, helping me see Jesus's feminine characteristics in a powerful way. Nevertheless, I spent the next few years convinced that Jesus's assigned male gender meant that the Christian God is definitively male. My lens was still clouded by whitemalegod who insists on God's maleness.

But my jaw dropped when I first heard Franciscan priest Father Richard Rohr explain the concept of the Cosmic Christ. Drawing from texts on the "Christ mystery" in the New Testament, he explained that Jesus and Christ are connected but distinct. Christ is the cosmic figure who exists in all spaces and time, whereas Jesus is a manifestation of the Christ figure in one historical and religious space. He writes, "We made Christ into Jesus's last name instead of realizing it was a description of [the Divine's] universal role in history."[27]

This new lens helped me understand that Christ's identity is not limited by Jesus's maleness. Yes, Christ came to Earth in the form of a man. But Jesus wasn't the only manifestation of Christ, nor was he Christ's only visit to Earth. Scholars agree that christophanies (Christ appearances) occur throughout the Judeo-Christian, Hindu, and Muslim scriptures, as well as in Indigenous spiritual narratives. For example, in Genesis 32, the angel who wrestles with Jacob is understood to be Christ.[28] Christ exists in many spaces and religions. So, to insist that the existence of Jesus means that Christ is exclusively male is like insisting that the existence of the dove messenger in the Noah's ark story means that the Holy Spirit is exclusively a bird. Through this new lens, I began to comprehend what the medieval mystics who honored the Divine Mothering in Christ understood long ago: one gender cannot exclusively represent the fullness of the mystery of Christ.

I eventually accepted the idea of a feminine divine, but the idea of a Sacred *Black* Feminine continued to elude me.

For example, I struggled to believe Douglas when she said "Christ is a Black woman whenever Black women act to establish life and wholeness for the Black community."[29] My whole life I had been exclusively exposed to white male images of God that implicitly but powerfully taught me that only white men could truly be made in the "image of God" and could truly be good. As a result, it was excruciatingly difficult for me to begin to see my Black female reflection in the holy Divine. And in typical white patriarchal fashion, I blamed the victim: myself. Over the years, as I struggled to attain and maintain a positive self-image, I often chastised myself for not easily silencing and rising above the negative messages I have received as a Black woman. I thought my persistent low self-image was a function of some character defect, as if I am to blame for simply believing what society had told me my entire life. Seeing myself in the divine seemed like an unattainable goal.

yet hope prevails

Whitemalegod's devastating impact on my Black female identity seemed irreversible, but all hope was not lost. Pinkola Estés offered me a glimpse of a different view of God, one that is neither white nor male. Speaking of the Sacred Black Feminine, she affirmed, "It is not by accident that she is called La Conquista, the Mother of the Conquered, for she pours her strength especially into us who have at least once in our lives been deeply stunned and staggered, harmfully shocked and pulled down, painfully intruded upon and left for dead.

Even yet, in the midst of all of the bandages and broken spirit-bones, she calls us to stop mis-thinking that we stand alone in our challenges, when in fact, she ever stands with us."[30]

Waking up to the reality of whitemalegod is deeply stunning. So, I clung to this truth about the Sacred Black Feminine as I staggered toward healing. As I began to face the terrible truth that the spiritual community of my origin lied to me about who God is, how God relates to me, and who I am, I lost myself in a storm of debilitating grief and rage. Even more, when I began to take seriously the truth that God is not white or male, I was swept away in a whirlwind of destabilizing uncertainty as questions I thought I had airtight answers to—*Who is God?*, *What is true?*, and *Where do I find spiritual community that is not patriarchal or anti-Black?*—simply led to more troubling questions—*Who am I?* and *Will I survive this?* Further, as I began to uncover the ghastly patriarchy and white supremacy within spiritual spaces and broader society, I began to understand that in order to truly encounter myself in the Sacred Black Feminine, I would need to fearlessly examine the whitemalegod in me. I would need to uncover and release all the ways in which I have adopted whitemalegod's ways, such as the obsession with certainty, perfectionism, and outside approval. I would also need to discern how my actions and beliefs have upheld whitemalegod's violent power structure. In order to believe that the Sacred Black Feminine truly lives within ALL of us, a lot that lived within me would need to die.

But I didn't have to encounter death all by myself. In early 2017, as I began researching different images of the

Sacred Black Feminine, one particular Black Madonna captivated me from the start. Our Lady of the Good Death is the queen of the massive black-rock gothic cathedral in Clermont-Ferrand, the capital of the Auvergne region of France. She is defiantly Blackity-Black. Her skin is so dark it radiates, and Her beautiful face illuminates a loving fierceness that I often see in the Black women I know and trust.

Since the 1100s, people have called her Our Lady of the Good Death because She is known for helping us die to our false selves—the counterfeit identities that are captive to society's expectations and beliefs about us. But She doesn't stop there. She also guides us to our true identity in the arms of the loving Sacred Black Feminine who is always available, always present, and always empowering. When we are most disillusioned and perplexed about who whitemalegod has shaped us to be, She helps us find our true center. Her title Our Lady of the Good Death offers immense hope because it promises that death yields restorative goodness. It assures us that if we take a tentative step away from the certainty of whitemalegod's oppressive reality and toward Her expansive, loving arms, we will experience a death that gives birth to true life. Not bound by rationality, She stands at the mystical intersection of death and life, empowering us to faithfully die to all that imprisons us so we can experience true life.

As I learned about Our Lady of the Good Death, I realized She would be my trustworthy companion, protector, and guide as I took my first, uncertain steps away from the trappings of whitemalegod. She would help me begin to awaken to the whitemalegod-induced behaviors that held me back from Her and She would invite me into new beliefs and practices that would set me free. I trusted that I would encounter Her in the lives and work of others seeking liberation and that I wouldn't have to journey alone. I began to see, as I loosened my grip on my familiar but faux identities, that Our Lady of the Good Death would help me discover my deeper identities. From the first stunned step and beyond, She would be there, guiding me toward life. As I awakened to whitemalegod, I was not alone.

Almost two years later, in late 2018, I finally traveled to the Auvergne region of France to begin my walking pilgrimage. As my plane began its descent into Clermont-Ferrand, I knew I had to see Our Lady of the Good Death first. I could not wait to meet the One who had helped me begin to die to the false self in which whitemalegod imprisoned me. As soon as my plane landed, I caught a taxi to my Airbnb and unpacked my roller duffle just enough to find my sneakers, sports bra, and leggings. Then I ran the one-mile distance from my apartment to the cathedral.

Breathless, I shoved open the heavy wooden doors and speed walked around the stadium-sized cathedral until I found Her in the sacrament chapel tucked behind the altar. When I saw Our Lady of the Good Death's dark, powerful body, I gasped and instinctively dropped to my knees.

As I looked up at Her, I encountered my journey within Her. In Her clear black eyes, I recognized my tenacity to look beyond what I thought I knew about God. In Her direct but gentle gaze, I saw that my search for the whitemalegod in me had been, above all, an act of self-love. In

Her sturdy, confident stature, I witnessed my courage to take seriously the truth that God is not white or male even if that meant turning my life upside down. As I kneeled before Our Lady of the Good Death, I encountered the Sacred Black Feminine who steadied my first staggering steps beyond whitmalegod's barren patch of certainty and into the mystical unknown. For hours, I gratefully sat with the One who powerfully invited me into the journey of death and life, basking in Her healing presence. As I walked back to my apartment, I knew this was only the beginning. Our Lady of the Good Death would continue to help me die so I could truly live.

If you're eager to go on this journey with me, you can trust that Our Lady of the Good Death stands with you and steadies you too. No matter your racial or gender identity, She is with you as you examine how whitemalegod has shaped you. She holds you as you die to your false selves and helps you relinquish the power you may have unjustly gained from them. And She guides you to your true identity in the arms of the loving Sacred Black Feminine who is always available, always present, and always empowering.

3

She Who Guides Us along the Freedom Path

In early 2017, just weeks into my awakening toward the Sacred Black Feminine, I dreamt I stood at the edge of a wealthy suburban development. As I faced the neighborhood, I surveyed the prosperous homes, perfectly paved circular driveways, professionally manicured lawns, expansive gardens, and energetic inhabitants. A picture of perfection. Yet, just beyond the neighborhood stood an eyesore—a vast, terrifying, uncultivated, and untamable forest full of briars, vines, trees, and bushes. There were no visible trails; the forest was simply an impassable mess.

As a '90s kid, I had watched the cult film *The Princess Bride* about a hundred times. The boundless thicket that lay before me conjured up images of the infamous Fire Swamp and its roaring fires, booby-trap quicksand, and giant human-eating rodents.

I shuddered.

Yet I was reluctant to redirect my eyes back to the suburban development because a glimmering light shone through the knotty thicket. And though the light was barely visible, I was instantly enchanted.

"What could be alive and full of light deep within this terrifying, pathless darkness?" I wondered.

As I peered more intently into the forest, I began to make out a faint, barely discernible path that led toward the captivating light. Intrigued, I leaned forward in an effort to help my squinting eyes follow the trail as far as they could. Just as I leaned in, the forest sprang to life! Sprigs of lavender magically sprung up along the path, their soothing scent filling the air and beckoning me forward. All around the path, dead-looking trees woke from their slumber and the scent of lavender soon began making melodies with the aromas of spicy balsam, minty eucalyptus, and zesty lemon trees. As I gazed upward, a roost of butterflies descended from the trees and moved down the path, tempting me to follow them toward the shimmering light. As I looked downward, fireflies illuminated the darkest corners, lighting my way.

Though the forest remained wild, it no longer scared me. Duly bewitched, I now wanted to discover the magic and beauty that lay deep within the forest, but something within me hesitated and I momentarily shifted my gaze away from the forest and back toward the suburban development. I wanted to take one last glance at all that I would leave behind if I ventured into the thicket. As I surveyed the neighborhood, another transformation occurred. Eyeing the roads, I noticed they all led to dead ends. There was no way to drive out of the neighborhood; any attempt to leave simply resulted in endless circling in what now appeared to be a creepy cul-de-sac hell. As I scrutinized the neighborhood, I noticed the robotic phoniness of the neighbors' obligatory hand waves as they fearfully installed their top-of-the-line home-security systems. The thin veneer of prosperity lifted and I began to see ruptures in the foundations of the homes, fences that sagged despite their owner's constant attempts to fortify them, cracks in supposedly unbreakable glass windows, and the lifeless eyes of people who worked tirelessly to obtain a sense of security that persistently eluded them.

As my gaze continued over the increasingly sad suburbia, several Confederatelike monuments of whitemalegod erupted from the ground, destroying the tidy cement pavement. The Confederate whitemalegods towered over the neighborhood, each one bearing a different brass plaque that paid homage to toxic masculinity's idols of knowledge: logic, reason, tradition, certainty, and consensus. The monuments continued to rise, blocking the sun and casting a gloomy pall over what had formerly seemed like a tony, optimistic, and safe enclave.

The violent whitemalegod eruptions abruptly awakened me from my slumber. At first bewildered, I gripped my sweat-soaked, tattered Dartmouth College T-shirt and realized it had all been a dream. Yet my rapid and pounding heartbeat told me that the whitemalegod monuments were real. I sat up in my bed and pondered the dream. I had a choice: I could follow the mystical, intuitive path toward life or stick to whitemalegod's barren but certain world with its over-reliance on logic, reason, tradition, certainty, and consensus.

Now that I was a few months into my conscious journey toward the Sacred Black Feminine, She was lovingly calling me to not just *argue* that God is a Black Woman, but to also *embody* the Sacred Black Feminine. You see, I was good at the arguing part. Really good at it. As a social psychologist, theologian, and professor at Duke University's Divinity School, I had mastered the masculine ways of knowing and could easily defend my journey toward the Sacred Black Feminine. I had conducted extensive academic research on the divine feminine and could cite famous church saints, such as Julian of Norwich, who affirm that God is mother. I could make a logical, social science–based argument that the Sacred Black Feminine is a necessary antidote to the ills of white patriarchal religion. I could give thoughtful lectures on the history of the Black Madonna and draw upon the work of well-respected theologians as I argued for the legitimacy of the Sacred Black Feminine.

And I had plenty of opportunities to argue for the legitimacy of the Sacred Black Feminine. As people in my spiritual and academic circles caught wind of my public musings about God's race and gender, my inbox filled with questions and accusations.

"How can you claim that God is female when Jesus was so obviously male?"

"But how do you know *that God is a Black Woman? Prove it."*

"Are you a witch?"

In response to these questions, I spent a ridiculous amount of time justifying my beliefs and framing them through the lens of traditional Christianity. But my dream invited me into something beyond the so-called acceptable ways of knowing, teaching me that the Sacred Black Feminine cannot be distilled into a TED Talk or a tidy sermon. Though She can rock with the best of the intellectuals, She exists beyond the edges, beyond the orthodox ways of knowing, and beyond traditional logic. She beckons us in dreams and speaks to us through our embodied experiences. As I continued to journey toward the Sacred Black Feminine, I could see that She was guiding me away from my obsession to *prove* Her and instead inviting me to simply *experience* Her.

Indeed, Pinkola Estés traveled the world to gather data about people's experiences of the Black Madonna and concluded that She stands "at the dividing line between waking consciousness and dreaming consciousness . . . taking in the two worlds, the mundane world of known facts, and the deeply creative, insightful, emergent world of Spirit."[1] In whitemalegod's hypermasculine world of reason, tradition, and certainty, the Sacred Black Feminine is entirely otherworldly, declaring Her truth not just through ideas but through magical and expansive experiences. Unlike whitemalegod, who is held hostage by logic, She also dwells in the feminine realm of intuition, possibility, and mysticism.

As I continued to reflect on my dream, I realized that She was mystically ushering me toward my Black female sacredness and divine right to be free. In the dream, I began to see that the light deep in the forest was a metaphor. As long as I stayed in the whitemalegod realm of reason, I would never be able to fully experience the Sacred Black Feminine, nor would I be able to argue my way to freedom. According to those parameters, my Black female soul would never be free. Similarly, since She dwells beyond the limited realm of head knowledge, mere knowledge of Her would never be enough to help me embody my sacredness or liberate myself. Only by experiencing Her can I fully embody my Black female sacredness and walk toward freedom.

The beautiful thing is that I began to experience the magic of the forest as soon as I began to release whitemalegod's idols of reason and tradition and moved toward Her guiding light. I didn't have to reach the light or prove the light's legitimacy before I experienced its magic; I simply had to begin to move toward it. As soon as I stepped into the seemingly dead forest, the magic of life erupted. In the same way, I trusted that by taking just one experiential step toward Her, I would begin to see Her sacred beauty within myself, others, and the world around me. In doing so, I quickly learned that each step empowered the next. Unlike fatherskygod who is *out there*, the Sacred Black Feminine is *right here* in the lavender aroma, the butterflies, the twinkle of fireflies, and within us. She abides in a magical world where dead forests spring to life when we choose to enter them because She dwells within us and our mere presence ushers in Her sacred and liberating life.

Black Women Just Be Knowin'

For centuries, Black women have eschewed tradition, consensus, and so-called legitimacy in favor of experiences that best honor their sacred selves and set them free. Indeed, Black women often dwell in the Sacred Black Feminine forest of intuition, possibility, and mysticism. For example, during the period of colonial enslavement, many Black women held *hush harbor* meetings—secret, illegal, after-dark gatherings during which they harvested the most life-giving elements of Christianity and combined them with ancestral African religious practices and avant-garde spirituality. Not willing to be confined to the barren and anti-Black world of the plantation church's white christ, the Black women of the hush harbors moved beyond the world of tradition, reason, and consensus and created their own magical spiritual world that affirmed their Black female embodied souls and offered them the hope they needed. Rather than allowing the white patriarchal establishment to dictate what is true, they relied on their own embodied wisdom. Beneath all the white christ propaganda that the enslaved Black women were forced to ingest, lay a deep, experiential *knowing* of a God who saw, affirmed, and liberated them.

The innovative and courageous tradition of hush harbors continues today in the work and lives of the *womanists*, a collective of Black feminist scholars, artists, parents, and healers who are fed up with the patriarchy inherent in the Black Liberation movement as well as the white supremacy that colonizes the feminist movement. The womanists don't give a shit about the consensus or the Church's beliefs or what the sacred texts *supposedly* say. Rather, they prioritize Black women's *lived* experiences above all other sources of knowledge.

The womanists don't care what whitemalegod and his minions think. They do not need to prove that their beliefs are in accordance with tradition. They are not looking to white patriarchy to affirm the legitimacy of their conclusions. Rather, they know they can trust their Black female perspectives on the world, the divine, and truth. And like Old Katerin, who insisted on searching for the Black Madonna in the ashes, the womanists will stop at nothing to find the One who identifies with and centers their particular experiences as Black women, the One whose proclamations are in favor of Black people's and women's liberation, the One who is unequivocally pro-Black and pro-woman.

Though whitemalegod's society devalues Black women's embodied experiences, truth, strength, and wisdom, womanism prizes them above all. According to anthropologist Linda Thomas, *womanism* is all about believing that Black women are sacred and that their *lived* experiences are the most important source of information as they determine what is true, what is valuable, what is hurtful, and what is healing, etc.[2] Womanists ask, "What nurtures hope in Black women? What is life-giving to Black women? What heals Black women? What liberates Black women? What helps Black women love themselves and their communities well?" The answers to those questions and others help womanists know what is Good News and what is not, what is good and what is evil, what is true and what is false, what is divine and what is not, and what is love and what is not. Above all, womanism proclaims that Black women and their perceptions, intuitions, and wisdom are sacred too.

In the wake of my harrowing dream, I devoured dozens of books on womanist philosophy, literature, and theology. Kelly Brown Douglas's *The Black Christ* exposed the ghastly white supremacist cracks in traditional interpretations of Christian scripture and set me free to walk away from the whitemalegod monument of Christian tradition. Jacquelyn Grant's *White Women's Christ and Black Woman's Jesus* was one big "Not today, colonizer" retort to white feminism that liberated me from trying to reconcile my experiences of the Black Madonna with white women's interpretations of Her.[3] But it was Monica Coleman's *Making a Way out of No Way*[4] that sent me lumbering into the magical Sacred Black Feminine forest. In her book, Coleman explains that as Black women forge their own path to the divine, they finally experience a God who sees and affirms them. That's exactly what I was looking for! Beneath all the whitemalegod propaganda I had ingested, I sought a deep, experiential *knowing* of a God who sees and affirms me. I sought a God who heard the terror in my Black female gut, helped me to see it as divine wisdom, and helped me to trust it.

The Womanist in Me

I desperately wanted to be a womanist. As I continued on my spiritual path toward the Sacred Black Feminine, I wanted to stop asking, "What can I prove? What is orthodox? What can be substantiated by history or scripture?" Instead, I wanted to begin asking, "What nurtures hope in my Black female embodied soul? What gives life to my Black female embodied soul? What heals my Black female embodied soul? What liberates my Black female embodied soul? What helps my Black female embodied soul love itself and others well?" I wanted to experience the world of the Sacred Black Feminine in which I trusted my experience and embodied wisdom more than reason and tradition.

But after years of academic training, I found myself trapped in my head. And after years of trauma, I was so disconnected from my body that I couldn't even begin to ask myself, "What feels hopeful to you, Christena?" And after centuries of enslavement, domestic servitude, and environmental racism, my Black female body was so severed from the Earth that I couldn't even imagine encountering the Sacred Black Feminine in a trail of butterflies.

She Who Guides Us beyond Fear and into Love

I had no idea how to begin to escape from whitemalegod's prison of the mind and embark on the mystical, embodied path of the Sacred Black Feminine. However, a trusted Black female friend suggested mindfulness meditation as a jumping off point. When I heard the word meditation, alarm bells went off in my Christianized mind and I flashed back to a scene in my childhood. As we drove by a hippy '90s yoga studio, my mom offered a disapproving grunt and warned me that "yoga and meditation are for people who think they can find peace outside of Jesus."

No longer willing to be confined to whitemalegod's monuments of tradition and orthodoxy, I shook Mom's words out of my body and immediately registered for a mindfulness class. *Mindfulness*, which means "maintaining a moment-by-moment awareness of our thoughts, feelings, bodily sensations, and surrounding environment, through a gentle, nurturing lens"[5] enabled me to start to *feel* the terror that I had been numbing since I was five. Our teacher Judith showed us that by paying conscious attention to our breath, feeling our body sensations as we scanned each limb, muscle, and vertebrae, and clearing our mind of intrusive thoughts we can learn to be present to our experience regardless of whether it is pleasant or unpleasant. In other words, I could learn to deal with the terror I was feeling without rushing to numb. I dove right in, eager to learn this new way of being.

But as I completed the daily home practices, the terror in my gut began to rise to the surface and I began to notice that it ruled my conscious experience. I was afraid of the death threats, afraid that I could never be sacred, afraid that my sister Des would never be accepted and nurtured by society, afraid that I would never heal from whitemalegod's terror, afraid that justice would never prevail, afraid that Black lives would never truly matter, and afraid that I could never truly be worthy. Fear was my loudest companion and the most rational emotional response to my ongoing experience as a Black woman. I needed an experience with the Sacred Black Feminine that went beyond rationality. I needed an experience of the Sacred Black Feminine that ushered me past the gates of fear and into the empowering world of mysticism, love, and hope.

One day in class, Judith shared the Buddhist teaching that Love and Fear form the basis of everything. In other words, every thought, emotion, and behavior come from either a place of Love or a place of Fear because they are the driving fundamental forces in the world. This teaching brought tears to my eyes and filled me with hope because it meant that if Fear was loud in my body, Love could be loud too. As someone who been held hostage by terror my entire life, I was desperate to be set free into the arms of Love. I knew in my heart that if I continued on my mindfulness journey, I would eventually uncover the Love that *had* to be buried beneath the fear.

About two months into the class, Judith invited the students to a day-long mindfulness retreat. Up until that point, I had only been practicing mindfulness meditation for about forty-five minutes a day, so an entire day of mindful silence intimidated me, but I went anyway because I was curious. Throughout the day, we remained silent and even avoided eye-contact as we tried to clear our minds of all thought by focusing our attention on our breath. At the end of the day, Judith invited us to try something different. "For this last period of meditation," she said, "instead of trying to clear your mind of your thoughts, feel free to welcome your thoughts. Just notice what happens when you open the floodgates."

I was scheduled to be a guest preacher at an evangelical megachurch in San Jose, California, in just two days. Upon hearing Judith's instructions for this last meditation period, I silently cheered and said to myself, "Oh, goody. Since I've been so disciplined at meditating all day, I bet God will download all sorts of dazzling wisdom on me right now so I can impress the people in my sermon on Sunday." As someone who had been raised in whitemalegod's society, I was fixated on my performance and my worthiness to others. I couldn't imagine that I was unconditionally sacred and worthy of a good gift mystically offered just for me.

I sat cross-legged on my mat, and as soon as I closed my eyes and turned inward, a wave of Love crashed into me, a wave so formidable that it forced my upright body backward and onto the floor pillows behind me. The overwhelmingly powerful force was distinctly pleasurable, but had it been any stronger, it would have been physically painful. This was a mighty force that didn't abuse. It was force without manipulation, force without control, and force without shame. It was the force of Love—a force I had never encountered in whitemalegod's world. I knew I couldn't fight the powerful waves, and as I felt my shoulders expand onto the pillows, my neck muscles relax, and my legs unfold and extend themselves, I realized my body didn't want to fight. So, I lay surrendered for the entire meditation period as the potent waves relentlessly and lovingly pinned me to the floor.

I had never before experienced formidable strength in the form of Love and it undid me. I marveled that after an entire day of earnestly clearing my mind of fearful clutter, what lay beneath it all was not another to-do list from whitemalegod, or another hoop to jump through, or another bundle of resources to share with others in order to make myself useful. No, Love was underneath it all, just as I had hoped. That day, I discovered that at the heart of reality—beneath whitemalegod's maze of terrifying propaganda—flows wave after wave after wave of Love . . . for me.

If such formidable waves of Love are constantly flowing toward me, then I must be getting free, I whispered to myself.

As the waves pinned my Black female body to the floor, I surrendered to the Love. White patriarchy had chained me to fear for a long time, but it was simply no match for mystical Love.

This experience showed me that no matter what is going on around me and no matter how much fear tries to consume me, the Sacred Black Feminine is always available to guide me into Love. This truth sent me yearning for more connection to myself, the Earth, and the Sacred Black Feminine. After the retreat, I continued my academic research on the Black Madonna, but I also jumped headfirst into mindfulness practice and intensive trauma therapy. In an effort to connect more deeply with my body and the natural world around me, I also began a contemplative walking practice, going for long five- to fifteen-mile walks that quieted the "shoulds" in my head, got me to slow down, and encouraged me to simply be present to all around me and within me.

Before long, She guided me beyond the need to prove the Sacred Black Feminine's legitimacy. Instead, I relaxed into my embodied experience of Her, which reliably quieted my fears, opened me to love, and nurtured my hope. Though the accusatory messages continued to fill my inbox, I remained unbothered. When people queried "Are you a witch?" I simply responded with "I might be . . . BOO!"

She Who Guides Us into New Ways of Being

The combination of contemplative walking, mindfulness meditation, and academic research created an explosion of magical encounters with the Sacred Black Feminine. As I deepened my understanding of Black Madonnas all over the world, I discovered a constellation of liberating images that gave life to my spiritual imagination and guided me beyond whitemalegod's barren patch of certainty, tradition, logic, and consensus. This is no surprise, for as Pinkola Estés writes, "The province of the Black Madonna appears to be, in large part, to urge the human spirit to inquire and see beyond the 'expected,' beyond what is considered to be the 'only way to properly see,' to grasp the greater picture beyond that which is most easily perceived by ego alone."[6]

The same urging in my own human spirit birthed a desire to visit the Black Madonnas with both my mind *and* body. That's why, as I planned for my pilgrimage in 2018, I decided to make my Black Madonna pilgrimage a *walking* pilgrimage in the Auvergne region of France. Rather than remain trapped in my white patriarchy-trained mind, I wanted to connect with my intrinsic Sacred Black Feminine wisdom as I encountered the ancient Black Madonnas. I wanted to get out of my mind and into my body so I could continue to integrate as the Sacred Black Feminine so beautifully does. I wanted to move at a slower pace so I could take the time to notice how my feet landed on the leaf-covered ground, listen to the rumble in my stomach, and honor my sacred body by taking breaks when needed. I wanted to attend to the whistle of the wind, rest my head against the gnarled bark of trees, take in a whiff of budding wildflowers, and caress the lava rocks from which so many of the Black Madonnas of the Auvergne were formed. I wanted to be able to encounter each Black Madonna and say, "I walked dozens of miles, took thousands of breaths, met scores of people, and listened deeply to my body and to nature in order to meet you." Above all, I wanted to *experience* the Sacred Black Feminine so that I could find myself in Her and be free to embrace my sacredness too.

She Who Guides Our Sacred Steps

Not long after I began my pilgrimage in France, I day tripped to Moulins, a small city about sixty-five miles from Clermont-Ferrand. Still jet-lagged and not feeling quite ready to walk the entire journey, I took a train part of the way and walked the remaining eleven miles. I was already beginning to listen to my body and honor my needs.

The city of Moulins is truly enchanted. A romantic river walk and mazes of cobblestone streets surround the medieval cathedral, inviting me to wander the bustling alleys, peek into tea shops lined with hundreds of shiny black cannisters of exquisite tea, purchase a cheery red and green shirt from a Senegalese merchant, and sit by the expansive Allier river breathing in the cutting fall air. As I walked the city, I was taken aback by the vast number of statues and monuments that filled the urban squares, staked their claim on street corners, and even adorned the exterior of the gothic cathedral. Everywhere I turned, I encountered a stone, marble, or bronze likeness of a church saint, French royalty, or military commander. Don't get me wrong, every French city has lots of statues and monuments; the French love their traditions and history and are really extra about them. But Moulins was one of the most important art centers of the early

Renaissance period so it uniquely bursts with monuments and statues.

When I finally entered the expansive Moulins cathedral, I encountered even more statues and monuments—scores of them! I had never seen so many in one place before and I was reminded of the whitemalegod monuments in my dream. The overwhelming number of historical statues and monuments seemed to crowd the spiritual space and diminish its present-day usefulness. Though one can easily get lost among the many statues and monuments, it is impossible to miss the Black Madonna of Moulins. A sight to behold, She boldly stands out among the white male saints and white madonnas. Though She is over a thousand years old, there is nothing fragile about Her. In fact, the thick grayish-black paint that covers Her wooden body gives the appearance of Knights of the Round Table–style armor. And while many of the medieval Black Madonnas are small, She stands almost three feet tall. Beyond Her height, She appears even more commanding because Her seat is supported by a massive altar. Like a general on a horse, She stands head and shoulders above mere mortals. In order to gaze at Her, I had to look up, up, up.

It's no surprise that the Black Madonna of Moulins is such a fierce, divine creature. She is the Black Madonna to which Joan of Arc prayed in 1429 before she began her freedom fight for the lives and dignity of peasants and other oppressed people. As I stood before this Black Madonna, I wondered if Joan of Arc trembled in her boots as she stood in this very place before she went to battle. I wondered if Joan of Arc questioned the legitimacy and purity of her quest. I wondered if Joan of Arc questioned whether she was sacred too.

I'm certain Joan of Arc carried these fears and questions because she was human and whitemalegod was just as active in the 1400s as he is today. As the patron of white patriarchy, whitemalegod sits atop a precarious hierarchy. Like the white slaveholders, whitemalegod knows his dominance is illegitimate and that, at any minute, he could be facing a major uprising from the people he has long terrorized. As such, he is obsessed with maintaining our oppression, silence, timidity, and perpetual captivity. He wants to keep us in our tiny, disempowered identities and prevent us from moving forward on our liberation journey. One way he does this is by gaslighting us—causing us to question our perspectives on injustice, the legitimacy of our journeys, whether we can trust our hearts and desires as we break free, whether we're on the right path, and whether our experiences, stories, and voices are worth the battle. In short, whitemalegod wants us to question whether we are sacred too.

Just as the white slaveholders didn't want the enslaved African people to see themselves in Christ the Liberator, whitemalegod doesn't want us to encounter ourselves in the Divine. He knows he can no longer gaslight us if we understand that we are sacred too. He knows that when we embrace our right to be free, we will begin to trust our perceptions, including our sense that the system is fucked. He knows that when we embody our divinity, we will start to believe we deserve better than the crumbs white patriarchy tosses at us. We will begin to believe that our freedom is worth fighting for no matter the cost and that our tactics for liberation don't require his stamp of approval. He knows that, like Joan of Arc, we will believe it is our birthright to RISE UP and fight for our liberation.

As I stood before the Black Madonna in Moulins, envisioning fourteen-year-old Joan facing off against the oppressive powers of her day, I was reminded of a Joan of Arc quote affixed to the wall in my home office back in the US: "I am not afraid; I was born for this."

Just a few weeks before my pilgrimage, I spotted this quote on a trendy-looking poster in a chic-but-minimalist coffee shop in my hometown. Despite the hipster trappings, I immediately fell in love with the epic message and eagerly paid an exorbitant amount of money for the poster.

"I am not afraid; I was born for this."

Mounted above my writing desk, I felt like I received a pep talk every time I glanced at the poster. Like, *yeah, I can do this liberation journey! I can be strong! I can be brave! I can trust myself! Two, four, six, eight . . . who do we appreciate? Christena! Christena! Christena!*

But I later learned that the quote is inaccurate, that it had been truncated and despiritualized in order to appeal to a wider audience. What Joan of Arc *actually* said was:

> I do not fear the soldiers, for my road is made open
> to me; and if the soldiers come, I have God, my Lord,
> who will know how to clear the route . . . It was for
> this that I was born![7]

So really, a more authentic summary of Joan of Arc's words is: "I am not afraid *because God is with me*. I was born for this!"

This version is so much more than a razzy cheer. It's more than a motivational slogan or self-help tidbit. It's an entirely different way of envisioning and relating to the Divine. Since identity isn't just an individual thing, our identity is transformed when we reject the distant fatherskygod and begin to see ourselves in close proximity to the Divine. Social psychology teaches us that people are social animals who are shaped and formed in the context of their social situations. Early sociologist Charles Cooley understood the self to be a "looking glass,"[8] which is just an old-timey word for mirror. By calling the self a mirror, Cooley was showing us that we come to understand ourselves by noticing how people perceive us and interact with us. In other words, people's reactions to us influence how we understand ourselves. If people respond to us and treat us like we are intelligent, we begin to identify as intelligent. If people respond to us and treat us like we are criminals, we begin to identify as criminal. If people respond to us and treat us like we are beautiful, we begin to identify as beautiful. If people respond to us and treat us like we are divine, we begin to identify as divine.

But whitemalegod seems to hold all the mirrors in our society. Everywhere we look, our perceptions of self and gender and racial identities are terrorized by the racist, sexist, and transphobic values of whitemalegod, who can only truly affirm the divinity of straight, cis white men and the tiny number of people they deem acceptable. Under this lens, it's no wonder that a Black woman like me struggled to connect with my divine intuition. Just like my enslaved African ancestors, I had been taught that God wasn't anywhere to be found in me, and that my only hope was to accept the dehumanizing remnants that white patriarchy handed me.

However, the Black Madonna of Moulins's Black female body makes a bold statement about God's social location, declaring that She is *with* Black women and relates to Black women. Just like whitemalegod's white male body affirms the dignity and sacredness of white men, the Sacred Black Feminine's Black female body affirms the dignity and sacredness of Black women. But by affirming the dignity and sacredness of Black women who are among the most marginalized in society, She also affirms the dignity and sacredness of all people. For if society's least sacred are made sacred by Her identification with them, then truly all are sacred. Unlike whitemalegod, the Sacred Black Feminine doesn't exclude anyone from Her holy huddle. Though She specifically declares Black women to be sacred, She affirms the sacredness of all.

As Joan of Arc, a white woman, can attest—our identities soar when we begin to relate to a God who calls us sacred. Joan of Arc was able to face off against the oppressive powers of her time precisely because She knew that the Divine was *with* her. Joan of Arc didn't have to struggle to trust her gut nor did she question the legitimacy of her quest for liberation. She knew it was divine because the Divine was *with* her.

The Black Madonna of Moulins sees us and identifies with us. Never again are we to be called unholy or distant from the Divine. She is wholly holy and She's the one holding the mirrors now, reflecting our sacredness. Now that we know we are sacred, we can hold our head high. We can stand up for what we believe in. We can trust our intuitions as we travel along the freedom path. We can see our bodies as divine gifts and trustworthy sources of wisdom. We can cherish ourselves. We can trust that we are not alone as we fight for our freedom. The Sacred Black Feminine stands with us, guides us, and calls us sacred too.

But Is She Black Tho'?

I like my heroes as I like my identities—intersectional. Though I appreciate the story, Joan of Arc's encounter with the Black Madonna of Moulins doesn't quite do it for me. I get that she's a feminist icon. But I rarely encounter myself in the stories of "heroic" white women because they don't relate to my intersectional identity as a Black woman. And if white feminism has taught us anything, it's that white women's "heroism" often hurts Black women because white women benefit so much from whitemalegod's anti-Blackness. Besides, it's specifically *Black* women who whitemalegod has condemned as opposite of the Divine. We're the ones who've lumbered under the weight of the enduring Jezebel stereotype.

As a budding womanist, I knew I could defiantly prioritize my embodied experience and needs as a Black woman over tradition, history, and other whitemalegod ways of knowing. As a budding mystic, I knew I could ask myself,

"What makes me feel hope here? What is life-giving to me? What is liberating to me? What do I need?" Having just encountered the wholly holy Black Madonna of Moulins, I knew I could trust my divine intuition to guide me beyond the suburban development of reason and into the magical forest of possibility. Further, to be honest, I *needed* to know that the Black Madonna of Moulins is not just with white women like Joan of Arc. I needed to know that the Black Madonna of Moulins is with Black women.

As I gazed at the Black Madonna of Moulins, I began "making a way out of no way" beyond Joan of Arc's story. No white woman, no matter how heroic or iconic she is, could possibly fully embody the Sacred Black Feminine–warrior energy of this magnificently fierce Black Madonna. No, this is a job for a Black woman—someone who, unlike white women, truly understands what it means to be the anti-whitemalegod, the opposite of all that society holds valuable, true, and divine. With this prompt, it didn't take long for Harriet Tubman to blossom in my spiritual imagination. For I was certain that if Harriet Tubman had prayed before a Black Madonna statue, it would have been the magnificently fierce Black Madonna of Moulins.

Harriet's story offers a quintessential example of how the Sacred Black Feminine mothered, liberated, encouraged, emboldened, accompanied, and sustained her as she helped hundreds of people escape plantations. Though she's often remembered in mythical StrongBlackWoman-on-steroids proportions, Harriet lived under whitemalegod's oppressive rule too and was human too. Like Joan of Arc, she probably

questioned the legitimacy of her freedom, rights, and eman-
cipatory missions. Like me, she likely needed to heal her
Black female identity from years of whitemalegod's conditioning. Like me, she probably questioned her sacredness.
Like me, she likely feared she wouldn't be able to continue,
that she wouldn't find her strength, that she wouldn't find
her way.

Just Follow the North Star

Harriet often directed recent escapees to keep their eyes on
the North Star as they took their first steps toward freedom.[9]
To be sure, this was, in part, a navigational strategy. Since
most escape attempts took place under cover of night, it was
easy to lose one's way even in familiar territory.

However, as I stood before the sustaining, guiding power
of the Black Madonna of Moulins, I saw Harriet's connection to the North Star in a new light. The North Star, one
of the brightest stars in the galaxy and easy to spot from
North America, was a constant reminder of God's immanence. Unlike Joan of Arc, Harriet and the enslaved people
didn't have the luxury of stopping to pray to God in the
middle of their liberation journey. But they could keep their
eyes on the North Star—a constant reminder that they were
not alone, that God was with them as they rejected white
patriarchy and escaped to freedom. The North Star, like the
Black Madonna of Moulins, offered an image of the Divine
that related to their Blackness and to their fight for liberation. And the North Star reminded them that, despite what

white patriarchy had called them—Jezebel, uppity, unholy, stupid—they were sacred, and their mission was too. She guided them as they escaped to freedom.

Though Harriet Tubman is most known for *saving* hundreds of enslaved people's lives, she also *threatened* many enslaved people's lives.[10] Once an escape attempt had begun, Harriet would threaten to kill any escapee who tried to return to the plantation because their return endangered the entire group. By telling escapees to focus on the North Star, Harriet was giving them something on which to focus their attention. When they heard the gun shots and the dogs barking, when they feared for their lives, when their fear threatened to overtake them and send them back, when they felt compelled to return to the loved ones they had left behind, they simply needed to fix their focus on the North Star and allow it to guide them to freedom. The North Star was a reminder of what was true.

As I stood before the Black Madonna of Moulins, I realized that She was my North Star too. Not only was She a reminder that I was not alone, She was a reminder that, though I had no idea where I was going or how I would escape the many plantations on which I still remained, I needn't turn back. Instead, I could fix my eyes on Her so She could accompany me and embolden me as She did Harriet. I also realized that my entire four-hundred-mile pilgrimage to visit eighteen different Black Madonnas was my way of following the North Star to my freedom. At each stop on my pilgrimage, I came face-to-face with the immensely loving Sacred Black Feminine who intimately related to my experience as

a Black woman, and in whom I could discover my sacredness. Like the North Star, each Black Madonna reminded me
yet again that I am divine, that my quest for liberation is true,
and that I am accompanied as I fight the white patriarchy.
She is right there with me, affirming my wholly holy Black
femininity and guiding me to freedom just as She guided
Harriet. I clung to this truth as I returned to my apartment
in Clermont-Ferrand that evening.

At the time, I had no idea how much I needed to meet
my North Star in Moulins that day, for, as I would soon learn,
I needed to keep my eye on Her as I continued on the freedom path. I needed to keep my eye on Her as I began to plan
my escapes from the many whitemalegod plantations that
still littered my life. I needed to keep my eyes on Her when I
heard the gun shots and the dogs barking, when I feared for
my life, when my fear threatened to overtake me and send
me back into whitemalegod's inhospitable arms, when I felt
compelled to return to the loved ones I had left behind. I
needed to keep my eyes on the North Star and allow Her to
continue to guide me to freedom.

4

god of the gag reflex:
whitemalegod's disgust for human need

My buttocks began to quiver as soon as I spotted the shame in my dad's eyes. I knew I was in for a colossal beating.

Just minutes earlier, my Sunday school teachers Todd and Yvonne had inexplicably asked the students in the class to recite the vowels in the alphabet. As an adult, I am befuddled when I try to understand how knowledge of English vowels is relevant to spirituality, but as a five year old, I was simply eager to demonstrate my vast knowledge of the alphabet. Truth is, I was a kindergartener in desperate need of a win.

Kindergarten is supposed to be a fun foray into the formal educational world, but my life as a kindergartner had been cutthroat. A few months prior, I had transferred to a new class in public school—a kindergarten–first grade hybrid class— and I had struggled to catch up with my classmates in every subject but music. As the end of the school year approached,

I began to feel defeated. Every math calculation presented a conundrum, each phonetic pronunciation a puzzle. As I wrestled with my homework each night, I began to question whether I was capable of learning at all.

So, when my Sunday school teachers gave me a chance to show off my knowledge, my heart ballooned with hope. More than anything, I wanted to feel smart in a classroom setting—any classroom setting. I was more than willing to settle for Sunday school.

My mouth started moving before I even raised my bony, brown hand, "A-E-I-O-U-and-sometimes-Y," I self-assuredly declared.

The gleam of affirmation in my teacher Yvonne's eyes was balm to my beleaguered kindergartener heart. I beamed, eyeing the other students to make sure they understood how impressive I was.

Perhaps sensing my desperation, the co-teacher Todd chimed in, "Wow, Christena, you're so smart. That's amazing that a five year old can recite the vowels so perfectly."

Now I was hooked. This all felt too good. As far as I was concerned, Todd might as well have been the impossible-to-please landowner in the famous Bible parable we had recently learned about in Sunday school. This persnickety landowner typically criticized his servants' efforts but, in one case, he was so impressed with a servant's ingenuity that the landowner lavished praise on him, saying, "Well done, good and faithful servant!"

I could relate to the hard-working servant. After months of yearning and effort, I finally received the applause I craved!

Well done, good and faithful Christena! Naturally, I longed for more lavish praise, especially from authority figures like Todd and Yvonne.

So, I told a giant fib.

"Actually, I'm so smart that I'll be skipping first grade next year and going straight to second grade."

The room erupted in cheers and I felt cherished. I immediately hoped the feeling would last forever.

Unfortunately, it only lasted until the end of the Sunday school class. When my dad came to collect me, Yvonne mentioned to him that he must be so proud that I was skipping first grade.

"Christena . . . said . . . WHAT?" he stuttered. That's when I saw the shame in his eyes and knew that I was about to get a horrific beating. My fleeting experience of love was immediately replaced with fear and shame, both of which caused me to tremble as we drove the twenty miles home from church.

Dad seethed silently in the car. As soon as we arrived at our home, he said the one string of words that still makes me cringe today: "Get the stick."

I obediently lumbered into the house, climbed atop the washing machine in the central hallway, reached toward the shelf above the washer, and felt around for the thick rod that lurked at the poorly lit back of the shelf. My small brown fist clutching the thirty-six-inch stick, I hopped down from the washer and carried it to my dad, who was waiting for me in the place we always received our spankings—Mom and Dad's bedroom.

I knew the drill. Without saying a word, I lifted my Sunday dress over my shoulders and set it on the floor. Then I pulled off my cotton panties and carefully laid them on top of the dress. I kept my lace socks on because I knew that was allowed and I wanted to preserve any dignity I could. Undressed and bare-bottomed, I reluctantly turned toward the bed and lay down on my stomach. My naked back, butt, and legs were fully exposed to Dad and, before the beating even began, I felt shame.

I could hear the whip of the rod flying through the air, so I braced myself.

WHACK!

The rod barreled into my bare buttocks and I screamed in agony, "Daddy, I'm sorry! I'm sorry! Please stop!"

WHACK!

As my butt and thighs absorbed the exacting blow, the tears began to fall. Choking on my words, I twisted my body and faced my dad. Rod in hand, his arm was raised way above his head and shoulders, like a baseball pitcher winding up for a fastball. With my hands raised in plea, I cried, "Daddy! Please! Please stop! I'm sorry!"

Dad barked, "Turn over! Turn! Over!" Now that he was talking, he began to strike and talk in rhythm.

We . . . [WHACK] . . . do . . . [WHACK] . . . not . . . [WHACK] . . . lie . . . [WHACK]!

The severe agony in my butt spread to my entire body in spasmic waves—a torture tsunami.

We . . . [WHACK] . . . do . . . [WHACK] . . . not . . . [WHACK] . . . lie . . . [WHACK]!

I looked out the bedroom window, hoping to catch a glimpse of the blue afternoon sky, but I couldn't make out anything beyond a few inches from my face. As my head spinned, all I could see were stars.

We . . . [WHACK] . . . do . . . [WHACK] . . . not . . . [WHACK] . . . lie . . . [WHACK]!

It went on and on and on. I stopped screaming because my voice could no longer cry out. When it was over, but before I was allowed to get dressed, he told me to sit up and face him. Cringing as I placed my body's weight on my filleted butt and thighs, I sat on the edge of the bed wearing only my lace socks.

"I love you." He said. "You know this hurts me more than it hurts you, right? Let's pray together and ask God to help you learn from this." I couldn't comprehend his words. All I could understand was my shame, my pain, and my utter undesirability.

Legs buckling beneath me, I quietly gathered my clothes and slipped next door to the only bathroom in the house. Before I dressed, I surveyed the damage to my butt and thighs. Purple-and-black clouds the size of baseballs were already forming on my skin. At the time, I didn't know that it would be more than a month before I'd be able to walk without pain and more than three months before I would sit without wincing.

I wish my imperfection had triggered Dad's curiosity rather than his shame. I wish he had said to me, "Wow. You're a precious soul and you know it's important to tell the truth. What prompted you to tell a lie? What's going on? How can I help?"

Because he was unable to nurture my need, I was punished for having a very human need that I didn't yet know
how to express. During the beating, I received the messages
loud and clear:

It's not okay to need affirmation.

It's not okay to have a need.

Your humanity is shameful.

Your humanity is to be punished.

You're the problem; you made me hurt you.

*To be human is to be shameful; to be "good and faithful" is to
be perfect and needless.*

I was duly ashamed of my imperfect behavior and I re-
solved to never do anything that deviated from what my parents wanted me to do. In order to accomplish this impossible
task, I internalized my dad's critical voice and unleashed it
on myself. Whenever I was tempted to engage in behavior
that might be perceived as imperfect (e.g., breaking rules,
earning less than straight A's on my report card, forgetting
Bible knowledge, etc.), I shamed myself back into formation.

My efforts paid off. Not only was I rarely ever spanked
again, I became a shining example. My dad would often
boast to people, "Christena is the best Christian in the family." I was by no means a Goody Two-shoes; I was just more
effective than most at silencing my need. But in silencing my
need, I silenced myself almost to the point of self-erasure.

Even after I grew up and moved out of my parents' home,
it was many, many years before I discovered that my dad's abusive behavior toward me was a mirror image of whitemalegod's
abusive behavior toward all of humanity. One of the ways that

whitemalegod whips us into submission is by teaching us that we must conceal our human needs and imperfections in order to avoid punishment or social rejection. Due to my conditioning, it was years before I uncovered the liberating truth that my need is a luminous marker of my humanity. Our entire society is designed to conceal this truth.

whitemalegod's anti-nurturing world

Imagine a world where you are loved, valued, and safe. Can you describe it?[1]

In her book *Black Imagination*, artist Natasha Marin asked a multitude of Black Americans to respond to this prompt. The responses cast a vision of a world that is extraordinarily nurturing:

- "Sensitivity would return to the deepest reaches of us."[2]
- "I wouldn't need to put on my white woman voice to get bills paid . . . or discounts . . . or attention."[3]
- "My overall well-being is taken more into account than my amount of labor."[4]
- "We bring all of who we are."[5]
- "I would be a [racially] mixed Black Transgender Man . . . and still be soft."[6]
- "I wonder what tenderness is like, what it's like when the world doesn't exist to calcify my exterior, to prepare me for the blows to come, but rather cradles and protects so that the slightest scratch is unbearable."[7]

I yearn to live in a world like the one described in *Black Imagination*! Echoed throughout these imaginings is a desire to authentically express our needs and for them to be cherished by those around us. In other words, we long for nurturing, the kind of nurturing a loving mother gives a young child. We yearn for a society that beckons our most authentic selves and celebrates our glorious quirks and foibles. We long for a community that sees our need as an invitation to deepen our collective connections. We crave a world in which our humanity is honored first and foremost. We long for a sensitive society that grieves when a little Black girl believes she must lie about skipping first grade in order to receive affirmation.

But alas, the beautiful, nurturing picture portrayed above is a far cry from whitemalegod's society, in which patriarchy and white supremacy partner to proclaim that *to be human is to express no need*. In whitemalegod's society, toxic masculinity screeches "boys don't cry," young girls struggle to get dates after being labeled "high maintenance," and women are demoted for being "too emotional." Further, our infinitely vast gender diversity is squeezed into two suffocating male/female boxes in which men are more valued when they express no need, women are devalued precisely because they are often unable to adequately hide their need, and all other genders are completely erased unless they cram themselves into one of the two "official" gender boxes.

To need or not to need, that is how patriarchy determines who is valuable and who is not. No matter the gender, the more a person fits the mold of a needless "self-made man," the more they are celebrated. If you look at who sits atop the social ladder—in the corporate world, among a group of caregivers at the playground, within a spiritual community, on social media—you will find it is the people who excel at hiding their need. We worship those who seem to have it all together and make it "look easy." Everyone else is viewed as a liability and is shamed for being one.

The only time people in whitemalegod's world are allowed to talk openly about their need is when they are regaling themselves with tales of how they *triumphed* over it. We love to exchange stories about how we *used to be* homeless but now own a home with no mortgage on it, were *once* illiterate but now are a *New York Times* best-selling author, *used to be* an alcoholic but have been sober for twenty years, *once* struggled to manage our anger but now are a celebrated mindfulness teacher, *previously* had marital problems but now it's all good. In other words, it's okay to struggle, as long as you triumph in the long run. Just please don't tell us about your need in real time. Need is only acceptable in the past tense. We prefer the Hollywood version because it helps us disconnect from the shame we carry about our own needy humanity. Indeed, whitemalegod teaches us that we should be ashamed of our need because our need erodes all that is right and good in the world.

whitemalegod's intolerance for need

On Easter Sunday in 1989, I had the chicken pox and I was miserable. But there were no circumstances under which I, the child of preachers, was ever allowed to miss a Sunday service. So, I dutifully put on my white, lacy dress and white, ruffled socks and white, patent-leather shoes and sat alone in the last row so I wouldn't infect the other kids. Easter service at the Pentecostal church in which I was raised had the same vibe as a jubilant postwar victory parade. There was marching and dancing and trumpets and shouting and flags. Words like victory, conquer, and vanquish were prominently used to describe the finality of Christ's resurrection. Throughout the entire service, preachers-turned-cheerleaders exhorted us to energetically praise this God who had *once and for all* defeated death, sickness, and evil.

Despite the celebratory atmosphere, two questions nagged my little eight-year-old mind as I sat in my miniature quarantine at the back of the sanctuary:

How is it that I am sick if Christ has defeated sickness once and for all?

And since I am sick, does that mean that this victorious Christ is really far from me?

As a young kid, I wasn't conscious of my emotional needs. I couldn't have told you that I needed more affirmation or that I felt unsafe and lonely in my family home. But physical need was tangible and thus more understandable to my young mind. I understood that my unbearably itchy skin and fever fatigue meant that I had a need and I wanted someone to attend to it. I hated sitting all alone at the back of the church, disconnected from the celebrants who chanted about a God who had *defeated* the very need that I currently possessed. To this God, my need was irrelevant at best and deplorable at worst.

I felt shunned—not only by the people in my spiritual community, who were physically distant from me in the sanctuary, but also by the God, who was supposed to love me but clearly associated me with a threat that required his defeat. This cold and disapproving God seemed far from me and I blamed my physical need for his distance.

More than physically infected, I felt spiritually infected. The fact that death, sickness, and evil were all grouped together as the enemies of God led me to question whether my sickness meant that I too was an enemy of God. I had heard over and over again in church that if we just pray hard enough, God will heal us. I had prayed hard but to no avail. Now, sitting isolated in the sanctuary, I wondered if my persistent sickness was evidence of a deeper problem: an evil within me.

I could not bear the thought of being contaminated by evil and banished by God. So, I did what I had been taught to do in my home; I silenced my need and got into formation, hoping that in doing so I could regain a spot in the arms of my spiritual community and of God.

Taking a deep breath, I slowly pulled myself up off the pew and gingerly walked toward the celebration. As I approached the group, I began slowly clapping and moving my feet to the beat of the snare drum. A man smiled at me approvingly, patted me on the back, and handed me a tambourine adorned with colorful ribbons. I waved the tambourine high in the air, joining in on the worship of the God who had defeated sickness, even though I felt like shit and I longed to curl up in a mother's comforting arms.

needy people need not apply

Not everyone has experienced spiritual communities like the one in which I grew up. Nevertheless, many of us have received a similar message: in order to be considered worthy of love, value, and safety in whitemalegod's world, we must overcome whatever obstacles are in our way without displaying any need. Sociologist Shamus Khan uses the term *democratic inequality* to describe how we are tricked into believing that we all have the potential to be loved, valued, and safe in our society. Khan writes, "We live in a world of democratic inequality, by which I mean that our nation embraces the democratic principle of openness and access, yet as that embrace has increased so too have our levels of inequality."[8]

Khan's research shows that racial inequality has increased even though some of America's most elite institutions, such as Ivy League universities, have significantly increased in racial diversity. "We often think of openness and equality as going hand in hand. And yet if we look at our experiences over the last fifty years, we can see that that is simply not the case."

Indeed, in whitemalegod's house of mirrors, we are taught that any one of us can climb to the top where the wealthy white cisgender men hold court.

Everyone is welcome! Even a Black woman can be vice-president! says the wealthy, white, cisgender man.

But that's only true for the small percentage of us who are able to meet whitemalegod's exacting standards without expressing any need. The only people who "make it" are the ones who have access to life coaches, acceptable bodies and

clothing, legal aid, cultural knowledge, and other resources
that help them hide their need. Indeed, democratic inequality is a whitemalegod-shaped illusion. For example, econom-
ically oppressed Black women—who shoulder the triple
burden of white supremacy, patriarchy, and capitalism—
are labeled *Welfare Queens* if they dare rely on government
assistance.

Everyone is welcome, my ass.

Despite this obvious illusion, many of us scramble to disguise our human need as we chase the elusive acceptance
and false stability that whitemalegod offers. Though some
adults are successful at hiding their need, most kids are terrible at it. Some way or another, it rises to the surface, just
as it did when I was a distressed kindergartener. When this
happens, society reliably punishes them. Consequently, it's
no surprise that kids with greater needs are punished more
than other kids.

For example, research from the National Women's Law
Center shows that in all fifty US states, Black girls are suspended at least five-and-a-half times more often than white
girls, even though Black girls do not actually misbehave
more frequently or egregiously. If Black girls aren't more
mischievous and dangerous than white girls, then why the
disparity? The researchers explain: "Stereotypes of black girls
and women as 'angry' or aggressive, and 'promiscuous' or
hyper-sexualized can shape school officials' views of black
girls in critically harmful ways." As a result, Black girls are
punished for challenging what society considers "unfem-
inine" behavior, including being candid and assertive. The

researchers conclude that due to negative stereotypes about Black females, Black school girls' "assertiveness can often be misidentified as 'talking back' or 'defiance,' which puts them at greater risk for inequitable discipline."[9] When little Black girls speak out on behalf of their need, they are seen as a threat and punished accordingly.

disgusted by need

In whitemalegod's world, to be human is to be needless. So, of course, white patriarchy does not permit a definition of femininity that challenges the status quo. This is one way in which whitemalegod weaponizes femininity—by defining it as always silent and submissive to white patriarchy. In other words, if one has a need, one better keep it to oneself or only express it in ways that will not offend white patriarchy's fragile ego. This is a heavy burden for all women, but the weight is crushing little Black girls who, due to societal anti-Blackness and misogyny, carry great need in their bodies. Their societally inflicted need is LOUD and yet they are supposed to keep quiet.

Though Black girls' great need is a product of white patriarchy, Black girls are punished for *having* needs and then again for having the audacity to *express* their needs. When one's body is perceived as wholly unholy, as Black girls' bodies are perceived in whitemalegod's world, it doesn't take much for one's expression of need to be categorized as a threat.

This heart-crushing research illuminates just how much whitemalegod's society is disgusted by need. More than any other human characteristic, need seems to trigger white-malegod's gag reflex. This is not surprising given that white supremacy's value system is based on the toxic idea that perfection is the essence of legitimacy.

For centuries, the idea of whiteness has been mounted on a pillar of supposed purity and perfection. In 1781, Thomas Jefferson, one of whitemalegod's more prominent American minions, made it plain when he whitemansplained that whiteness differs from Blackness because whites are superior to Blacks by virtue of a number of human characteristics including physical beauty, intelligence, and the capacity to love.[10] By defining whiteness by its distance from Blackness and the "inferiority" of Black people, Jefferson equated whiteness with perfection and purity from "inferior" characteristics. So, to be white—and to be eligible for the love, value, and safety afforded to white people—is to distance oneself from the "imperfection" of Blackness. Because whiteness is forever captive to this toxic relationship with perfection, it is constantly chasing perfection and denying imperfection. Even more so, it is disgusted by need because it is a threat to white supremacy's claim of white racial superiority.

Whiteness's disgust for need is immortalized in the trophy of white masculinity: *the self-made man*. This mythical man who supposedly mastered his circumstances and acquired power in whitemalegod's world *all by himself* is celebrated in films, literature, and even historical accounts. The mythology of this rugged individualist looms large in whitemalegod's world, setting the standard for what it means to be human. The self-made man proclaims that not only is our need unacceptable, but we are expected to triumph over it without any significant help. We don't dare engage in vulnerable and mutual relationships with each other by admitting our need for help for fear that our vulnerability will allow others to dominate us.

This is how whitemalegod keeps us trapped—by convincing us that we must show no need if we want to be loved, valued, and safe.

the making of a needless father

I wonder what my dad, back when he was a young father, would have said if he had been asked to describe a world where he felt loved, valued, and safe. I wonder if he felt loved, valued, and safe at all. If he did, I couldn't see it through the raging shame in his eyes.

Shame was his trigger and, tragically, shame was perpetually locked-and-loaded in his soul. His story is one of resilience and humanity, but he couldn't see it that way. The favorite grandson of a celebrated bishop in the Church of God in Christ (COGIC), a Pentecostal denomination that prides itself on being "sanctified" in an unholy world, Dad was raised to strive for spiritual perfection. Though COGIC is predominantly Black, whitemalegod's anti-nurturing fingerprints are all over it.

But whitemalegod wasn't just confined to Dad's Black church community. As a Black boy growing up in the 1960s and 1970s in Watts, California, he understood that the broader white society could be just as punitive and anti-nurturing as the church. The message from society was clear and resounding: we will let you live if you act like Rev. Dr. Martin Luther King in his early years. In other words, we will let you live if you make no mistakes and contort your Black maleness into a figure that is acceptable to white moderates. But as a nine year old who survived the horrific anti-Black violence surrounding the Watts riots in 1965, he also witnessed what happens when Black people express need in a way that doesn't accommodate the white moderate's delicate sensitivities. Little Dad saw that when Black people ignored white patriarchy's rules of acceptability and spoke up loudly on behalf of their need, they were abused and annihilated by the very people who were supposed to serve and protect them.

At church and in broader society, the forces of white-malegod poisoned his developing identity, teaching him to conform to an unrealistic standard of needlessness and perfection. It wasn't long before Dad, a quick learner, internalized the idea of a punitive God who didn't tolerate human need, especially when the human is Black. So, Dad painfully contorted himself into a Black man that whitemalegod and whitemalegod's society could tolerate. Though he grew up in a socioeconomically oppressed neighborhood in Los Angeles and faced countless obstacles, he worked hard to make success "look easy." Perfection was his standard and it guided everything he did, including overcoming obstacles without ever expressing need. He was a self-made boy.

When his breadwinning father abandoned the young family for another woman, eleven-year-old Dad stepped up and became a surrogate father to his younger brother and an emotional companion to his mother, who was suddenly raising a family in poverty.

When the church organist was excommunicated for having an illicit affair, Dad's mom snapped her fingers and told him to "get up there and play." Even though thirteen-year-old Dad couldn't read music and had no experience playing *any* musical instrument, he hopped on the organ and began to play by ear. He remained the church organist until he went away to college.

When his high school's Friday night football games became the preferred battleground for the warring Los Angeles gangs, Dad, who was student body president, initiated and oversaw the process of moving the games from Friday nights to Friday afternoons. This upset the gang members, who threatened Dad at knifepoint in an attempt to get him to reverse the change. But Dad didn't flinch; the games proceeded on Friday afternoons, and the game time gang shootings ceased.

Throughout high school, Dad expertly concealed his need—always "beating the odds," shouldering unhealthy levels of responsibility, and denying his own right to be a gloriously imperfect human. As a young Black man in whitemalegod's anti-nurturing world, he coped by hiding his humanity behind the façade of resilient perfection. And in the end, he was rewarded with admission to Yale University and a bright future in whitemalegod's world.

My dad's story teaches us that, despite our best intentions, whitemalegod's disgust for our need has the power to infect us so severely that we pass the disgust on to our loved ones. Since at least the time of Thomas Jefferson, white-malegod has been crafting an alluring illusion that in order to be loved, valued, and safe, we must be needlessly perfect. Whether we realize it or not, we too have been infected with this lie and have become so disconnected from our true needs that we cannot recognize that the only time we feel loved, valued, and safe in society is when we imagine it.

And yet, we don't dare pause our panicked scramble toward perfection long enough to bravely face this truth, for to do so is to risk spiraling into shame as we ask ourselves why we can't be more like the needless people who seem to do it all and have it all. Indeed, whitemalegod dangles those people in front of us in the hopes that our shame will fuel our perfectionism and rid us of the human need he despises so much. But the seemingly needless humans who possess the prestigious diplomas, high-paying positions, spiritual authority, and social acclaim are simply a figment of whitemalegod's anti-nurturing world. Puppets in a hoax, they do not exist. Behind the branded platforms, pious pulpits, and prestigious podiums lies nothing but a vortex of shame that threatens to swallow us too. Every time we hide our need, we take one step closer to whitemalegod's contagious shame spiral and one step away from the liberating truth that our need is a luminous marker of our humanity.

As I awakened to the ways in which whitemalegod has shamed me into hiding my human need, I yearned to embrace my gloriously imperfect humanity. Further, I longed to help build a world in which little Black girls and young Black men and Black trans women and people of all races and genders are loved, valued, and safe. But I knew that if I didn't address my own shame-based obsession with perfection, I wouldn't be able to assist in creating such a world. Like my dad, I would remain trapped in my shame and destined to pass it on despite my good intentions.

I didn't know what the process would look like, but since I inherited my shame from whitemalegod, I trusted that somehow, someway, the Sacred Black Feminine could heal me. My faith did not fail me, for, as I would soon discover, one Black Madonna in particular powerfully showed me that the Sacred Black Feminine is especially equipped to reverse the shame that whitemalegod has forced upon us. For, if we are ever going to transform our woefully anti-nurturing society, we need a God who not only tolerates our human need but cherishes it. I encountered this God just months later on my pilgrimage to France. Her official name is Our Lady of the Sick, but I call Her *She Who Cherishes Our Hot Mess*.

5

She Who Cherishes Our Hot Mess

This much was clear to me: the Black Madonna of Vichy doesn't give a flying fuck about Thomas Jefferson and his toxic obsession with perfection. Though I had not yet visited Her, I instinctively knew She had nothing but side-eye for ol' TJ because (a) She is a Black woman and (b) desperate pilgrims have called her Our Lady of the Sick since the 1300s.

They didn't call her Our Lady of the Needless.

They didn't call her Our Lady of the Self-Made Man.

They didn't call her Our Lady of the Resilient Perfectionist.

They called her Our Lady of the Sick.

And that morning in France, Her mere name was music to my ears because I was sick as hell. Lying in my apartment in Clermont-Ferrand, I groaned and winced like it was Easter Sunday and I was a chicken pox–infected eight year old again. To make matters worse, I had spent the entire morning blaming and shaming myself for getting sick in the first place.

You see, two days earlier I had walked about fifteen miles to visit the Black Madonnas of nearby Marsat and Riom. One of my first long walks of the pilgrimage, I had eschewed the advice I had received about dressing in layers.

"Eh, I'll be fine without this thin windbreaker. How much can a skimpy little jacket make a difference?"

Apparently, a lot. About halfway into my walk, the November sunshine vanished, and the sky attacked me with a windy drizzle. Within an hour of walking in the rain, my fleece jacket and leggings were soaked through and my teeth began to chatter. With about two more hours of walking to go, I wished I hadn't been so stupid.

My inner critical voice continued yacking until I returned to my warm, dry apartment and then picked up again the following day when my nose started running. Fixating on my mistake and holding myself to an unreasonable standard of perfection, I kept criticizing myself.

"I'm only here for five weeks and I'm wasting precious time being sick. Now I won't be able to complete my long list of Black Madonnas and this trip will be such a failure. Not bringing my jacket was so stupid. I should have been better prepared. I don't deserve to have a successful pilgrimage."

The irony is that I decided to make my pilgrimage a walking pilgrimage precisely so I could slow down, connect more deeply with my body, and honor my gloriously human needs. The whole point of the walking pilgrimage was to listen to my body's needs and allow them, rather than my resilient perfectionism, to guide me. But my incessant self-criticism for getting sick revealed a deeper shame. I was ashamed that I was so late to this liberation journey. I was ashamed that I had stayed on the whitemalegod plantation for so long and I felt pressured to make up for lost time. Indeed, I was ashamed of my *need* for liberation. Whitemalegod capitalized on my shame, repeatedly taunting, "See, the *real* Black people began this journey a long time ago and they've left you behind. You'll never truly be free. It's too late and you're too far behind."

But after a day of being a walking megaphone for whitemalegod, the internal tornado became unbearable and I got fed up. Reminding myself that I no longer am compelled to listen to whitemalegod's disgust for my human need, I began to rack my brain for a truth to which I could pivot. That's when I remembered Our Lady of the Sick. I immediately sprang out of bed and ran into the living room to get my notes on Her.

The Needier, the Better

Much like Marvel superheroes, every Black Madonna has an origin story and is known for specific powers. Our Lady of the Sick is no different. Located in the heart of Vichy, France, She first came to people's attention because She lived right above a miraculous thermal spring. Sick and needy people from all over Europe and North Africa came to bathe in the spring and pray to the Sacred Black Feminine who stood just above it. Before long, reports of being healed at the spring and in Our Lady of the Sick's presence spread all over the world, and Vichy became *the* place to seek healing.

In the sixteenth-century, capitalism caught wind of the miracles and promptly colonized Vichy. Within just a few short years, luxurious Roman-style bathhouses designed to entice wealthy people to come bathe in the healing waters erupted all over the city. The most important people of the day, such as Napoleon III and the Pasha of Marrakech, often visited the Vichy resorts in search of healing . . . and also entertainment and gambling. Sometimes, at the end of their "Vegas weekend," the more devout rich people would swing by the statue of Our Lady of the Sick on their way out of town. Though She was no longer the city's main attraction, She generously welcomed them.

Yet, through it all, Our Lady of the Sick continued to receive sick and needy visitors, particularly the most desperate ones who could not afford entrance into the snazzy resorts. For those with great need, She was the only hope. Hundreds of thousands of peasants, African migrants, abused women, and neglected children traveled by foot across the Auvergne's Chaîne de Puys volcanic mountain range in order to dip in Her healing waters and speak to Her of their need. And the greater the need, the more She welcomed them. The people who experienced oppression loved Her so much that when Her statue was decapitated during the French Revolution, they tracked Her head down, built Her a new walnut body, and pieced Her back together.

I hadn't planned on visiting Her until later in the pilgrimage, but as I read through my notes, Our Lady of the Sick and Her pieced-back-together body called to me. I was overwhelmed by the image of the Sacred Black Feminine who looked like me and also beckoned my need. I immediately decided I needed to see Her. That day. Immediately.

Speaking aloud to the voice of whitemalegod within me, I imagined Thomas Jefferson, turned toward him, and declared directly into his white male, slaveholder eyes. "Nah, I'm through with you. Imma go with the Black Woman who has welcomed and comforted needy, marginalized people for hundreds of years."

Just envisioning Our Lady of the Sick energized me and the nausea and weakness left me. I got dressed, packed a lunch, and began the two-mile walk to the Clermont-Ferrand train station.

When I exited the train in Vichy, I immediately spotted the giant sixteen-foot statue of Our Lady of the Sick that serves as a steeple atop Her chapel. I breathed in relief, breathed out joy, and began the fifteen-minute walk to the chapel. As the steeple drew near, my pace quickened. I yearned for Her. When I could finally see the church building, I began to trot across the courtyard, half-walking half-skipping with excitement. I bounded up the stone steps of the church and burst inside. Entering the back of the church, I looked up at Her gloriously tall, walnut wood statue hovering above the altar at the front of sanctuary.

This time, I wasn't about to be quarantined in the back corner. Nothing was going to keep me from the Sacred Black Feminine who urged me to bring Her my needy self. I bum-rushed the altar and lunged toward Her. Wrapping my arms around Her legs, I was a toddler embracing her Mother.

I instinctively knew I was safe in the presence of the Black Madonna of Vichy, who beckons us to visit Her in all of our glorious human need. Unlike whitemalegod, no need disgusts Her. For centuries, the people most ostracized and hated by society—the people stricken with the plague, the genderqueer, the Black people, the serfs, the assaulted women, the people with grave physical and mental disabilities— all hovered at the open but unbroken circle at Her feet. She is the divine Black queen of the Island of Misfit Toys who declares that everyone belongs, *especially* the people that whitemalegod has cast aside for having the audacity to show their need.

Immanence is Her jam. She loves to get down into the thick of the human experience. *Nothing* makes Her gag or prevents Her from drawing near to us when we need Her most because, as a woman, She knows how society punishes women for having different physical needs than men. The late Black poet Ntozake Shange recognized how much white-malegod determines whose needs are sacred and whose needs are profane when she wrote, "We need a god who bleeds, [who] spreads her lunar vulva & showers us in shades of scarlet thick & warm like the breath of her."[1] Though not all women menstruate and not all people who menstruate are women, Our Lady of the Sick offers us a powerful image of the Sacred Black Feminine who can relate to all of the human experi-ence, even the parts that toxic masculinity shuns. She draws near to our human experience because it is Her experience too. She is a God who bleeds. Like a mother who stays up all night at the bedside of her sick child, Our Lady of the Sick is most present when our need is loud and messy.

In fact, the louder and messier, the better. It is impossible to overwhelm Her. As a Black woman, She knows how society punishes women who don't conform to the patriarchal standard of silent white femininity. She beckons the little Black girls who are suspended for having needs, gathers them in Her arms, hands each one a bedazzled megaphone and says, "Be loud, girls. I can handle your need, no matter how loud it is. Scream until your lungs no longer have wind. I'm here for you and I will never banish you."

As I looked up above Her giant statue, I gazed at the mural above Her altar. The mural depicts an elaborate dark, starry night, a lucid reminder that She also oversees the vast universe. Though She is immanent (right here) and gladly affirms and comforts our earthly concerns, She is also transcendent (out there). In addition to walking beside us, She travels a reality that our human minds cannot even begin to comprehend. Capable of juggling all the balls, She is both Queen of our grounded Island of Misfit Toys *and* Queen of the universe. We can confidently bring Her our needs and know that no need is too small to escape Her care or too vast to overwhelm Her. As Andrew Harvey says, "The full glory of the Mother is that she is at once both transcendent and immanent, the source of love and love-in-action."[2]

Our Lady of the Sick beautifully represents the relatable and reliable Divine Feminine that inspired the famous fifteenth-century Catholic prayer, ". . . never was it known that anyone who fled to your protection, implored your help, or sought your intercession, was left unaided."[3]

No longer quarantined in the back of the sanctuary, I knew that the Sacred Black Feminine had not left me behind. I knew I could bring Her not only my mild and temporary physical need, but also my megaphone-worthy needs, such as my need for freedom from perfectionism, self-criticism, and the voice of whitemalegod within me. Standing before a holy Black Woman who looked like She could be my biological mother, I didn't feel pressure to be anything other than my authentic, messy self. There were no tambourines to pick up, no jubilant songs to sing, no prosperity gospels to chant, and no hoops to jump through. Just me, Her, and my naked need.

In that moment, I was certain She would help me and that She would never abandon me. So, I told Her exactly why I had frantically run into Her presence. Spilling it all out on Her altar, I told Her how a minor misjudgment had stirred up a whitemalegod-sized shame tornado within me. I told Her I didn't know how to heal my aversions to imperfection and need. I told Her I didn't know how to stop shaming myself for staying on the plantation for so long. I told Her I didn't know how to surrender my needless independence and find my way back into Her firm hold.

I stopped abruptly. The last phrase shocked me, so I repeated it to myself: "*find my way back* into Your firm hold."

"Find my way back. Find my way back," I kept repeating to myself. I was remembering something. I hadn't always lived with an aversion to need. I was remembering a time when I used to trust that God cared about my need. I was remembering a time when I still frantically ran in search of Her. I was remembering a time before I settled for a white-malegod who despised my need.

Decapitated

When I was little, nothing energized me more than helping my dad. To be certain, part of my motivation stemmed from my desire to avoid awakening the whitemalegod-sized shame and punishment that slept lightly just beneath the surface of his soul. But like all humans, he was wondrously complex. He was as winsome and earnest as he was terrifying. Indeed, his generous, good heart often took center stage—and when that happened, I wanted to be just like him.

The ultimate "Daddy's Girl," I craved time with him. And since he was a busy bivocational minister, *helping* him was the best way to *be* with him. That's why the summer after I graduated kindergarten, I was up before dawn helping him staple some papers for his side hustle—teaching worker's compensation classes in the evenings. Eager to make myself useful, I worked as efficiently as I could, my petite five-year-old hands doing battle with a clunky, industrial-sized stapler. Before too long, the stapler bested me, sinking a staple deep into my thumb. I yelped and saw my thumb swell. Tears forming in my eyes, I frantically looked around for my dad to help me. But he was nowhere to be found; I guess he had temporarily left the room. Panicked and in agony, I did the best thing I could think of. I unlocked the front door, ran outside into the early dawn light, and sprinted toward Lillian's house.

Lillian was the friendly neighborhood mom. Warm and caring, she ran an in-home daycare and seemed to have an answer for every dilemma and a remedy for every ailment. I knew Lillian could help me . . . if I could just get to her. So, I ran and ran and ran—my bare feet thumping the cement sidewalk, my ruffled nighty blowing in the morning breeze, my other hand cradling my throbbing thumb as I crossed four streets to get to Lillian's house. By the time I arrived, my thumb was the size of my fist and my subdued sniffles had erupted into heavy sobs. Desperate, I ran across Lillian's wet, dewy yard and banged on her door. I feverishly banged and banged and banged. But Lillian didn't answer the door. No one answered. Exhausted and resigned, I turned around and walked slowly back to my house. On the way, I knew what I needed to do. I took a deep breath, cringed, and yanked the metal staple out of my thumb. In that moment, I learned what to do with my need when even the most nurturing person around isn't available. I learned to handle it all by myself.

We all learn this at some point in our lives. Whether it is because our pain accidentally fell through the cracks in a generally loving family, or because we are the victims of a strategic evil like sexual assault, transphobia, domestic violence, or ableism—we all know what it's like to feel alone in our need, to face real terror and know that no one is coming to help us. In our moment of greatest need, greatest exposure, greatest vulnerability, we frantically search for help but all we encounter is whitemalegod's anti-nurturing world, which scorns our need. So, we suspend our search for a God who welcomes our need, bunker down in whitemalegod's anti-nurturing regime, and stop putting our needs out there.

By the time I was five years old, I had stopped searching for Our Lady of the Sick. To cope in whitemalegod's world, I learned to "handle my needs" by silencing them. And in order to do that, in essence, I severed my head from my body.

"No pain, no need." I told myself. "If I just learn to ignore my pain, I won't have any need, and I won't be disappointed when no one nurtures me."

It started out in short bursts, like learning to silence great pain just long enough to pluck a staple from my thumb. But little by little, I learned to muzzle my pain in more lasting ways. With each beating from my dad, I learned to ignore the painful bruises on my buttocks and thighs because if I allowed them to telegraph my need, I would have to acknowledge it. I was willing to do anything to avoid needing a God who just wasn't there for me.

By the time I was in fifth grade, I had become so expert at ignoring my pain that when I fractured my ankle while fishing with my paternal grandad, I didn't bother to get it cast or even tell my parents about the injury. I just breathed through the pain and learned to live with it. I even completed my summer softball season without revealing my pain or expressing any need. The fact that our family lacked health insurance only supported my desire to silence my pain and need. As far as I was concerned, *if* God cared about my pain, he certainly didn't care enough to give us medical coverage.

A year after I broke my ankle, a driver in a pickup truck hit me while I was riding my bike in my neighborhood. Deathly afraid to display any need, I assured the driver that I was fine. But as I limped away, a caring bystander followed me home and told my parents about the accident. We still lacked health insurance but my dad called in a favor with an orthopedist he knew through his worker's compensation side hustle. When the Xray revealed I had broken my ankle about a year earlier, the doctor was incredulous.

"Did you know you broke your ankle recently?" he asked. "It looks like it was never cast."

"Yeah," I shrugged. "Can I go now?"

I knew how to handle my pain, and I certainly wasn't looking outside myself for help. I already knew that my expression of need would just result in major disappointment. No pain, no need.

Silencing my physical pain was an on-ramp to silencing my emotional pain. The deeper pain behind my physical injuries were emotional ones: the danger and abandonment I felt in my own home, the paralyzing fear I experienced when I realized we lacked healthcare and other social safety nets, and the terror that no one—not even God—was coming to help me. I coped with this emotional pain by ignoring it. Before long, the distance between my head and body became so great that I couldn't recognize my emotional pain. Like my father before me, I had no pain and I needed nothing. In the end, I did become just like him.

She Who Pieces Us Back Together

As I replayed these childhood memories at the altar of Our Lady of the Sick in Vichy, France, the symbolism of Her own decapitation overwhelmed me. As I spoke to Her of my own severed head and body, I cherished the fact that She represented an image of the Divine that understood my particular pain. Like me, She had been separated from Her body for years. And like me, She had been pieced back together.

I knew I could tell Her my messy truth: that I was barely pieced back together and that I was often at war with my embodied need. I knew I could tell Her that my healing journey was fitful at best. I knew I could tell Her that even after years of trauma therapy and mindfulness meditation, it still often feels like my body, emotions, and heart are miles away from my overdeveloped, overeducated, over-linear brain. I knew I could tell Her that even though I had embarked on this long walking pilgrimage precisely so I could reconnect with my gloriously imperfect humanity, I had allowed a small human error to trigger a self-attack. I knew I could tell Her that every step forward is followed by two steps back. I knew She understood because She too had been severed and She understood that the process of being pieced back together is a sacred weaving that cannot be rushed. Her story of being healed years after being decapitated was proof to me that my healing does not have a deadline and that every step in any direction belongs.

As I stood before Our Lady of the Sick, I realized I could *be* sick without hiding it. I could *be* stapled, *be* fractured, *be* afraid, *be* ashamed, *be* disappointed. As I stood boldly in my need, I comprehended that She wasn't playing when She arrived on the scene in the 1300s and said, "Y'all can call me *Our Lady of the Sick.* That's who I am and that's who I'm here for."

And the piecing back together begins by accepting that She loves our decapitated humanity as is. We begin to heal when we walk our unhealed selves up to Her altar and share our need.

As I offered Her my shame for staying on whitemale-god's plantation for so long, She helped me see how much shame I had been carrying and showed me I could offer myself compassion in light of that shame. As I stood before Her expansive, cosmic altar, I began to speak kindly to myself:

"*Of course* I felt paralyzing shame!"

"*Of course* I wondered if another way of life was possible."

"*Of course* I questioned whether my humanity mattered."

"*Of course* I betrayed myself by staying on the plantation. It was all I knew. My entire spiritual world was teaching me to betray myself; even its god was teaching me to betray myself."

"*Of course* I chose the false security of the plantation over the unknown. Fear was my teacher, my god, and my community."

Our Lady of the Sick's unconditional healing power empowered me to piece myself back together with self-compassion.

Our Lady of the Sick among Us

Pain notwithstanding, so much of our desire for physical, mental, and emotional healing stems from our desire for society to care for and nurture us. Our collective global experience of the COVID-19 pandemic attests to this truth. In whitemalegod's society, to have need is a social death sentence and is the best way to be excluded from any safety nets that are available. In particular, the elderly, people who live with chronic physical and/or mental illness, the disabled, and non-male people of color can attest to the fact that our anti-nurturing, inaccessible society shuns them and scorns their need. When we seek physical healing, we are not just looking for physical wellness. We are also looking for social acceptance and access to the goodies that whitemalegod only reserves for the needless.

At Her altar, everything belongs, but our need is our special offering to Her. You see, unlike whitemalegod, She welcomes our need because it reminds us to seek Her out. She knows that we're much more likely to bypass Her healing spring when we have the resources to numb our needs at the swanky spa across town. She knows She offers something the swanky spa can never provide. She knows that only Her unquestioned, undeniable, unavoidable, unconditional love can piece us back together after whitemalegod's society has decapitated us.

At Her magical spring, She redefines the concept of healing. She doesn't promise to eradicate our need (so we can then fit into whitemalegod's concept of who's valuable). Instead, She offers to heal our relationship to our body. She reconnects our head and body so we can know how we feel and what we need, begin to ask people for what we need, and start to build communities based on meeting need rather than scoffing at it.

In fact, Our Lady of the Sick exists most powerfully in our collective communities. Her matriarchal leadership inspires us to co-create the healing springs we need. We become Her when we work together to share and meet needs. Our Lady of the Sick lives on in communities that see need not as something to be silenced but, rather, something to be proclaimed.

Before beginning my journey toward the Sacred Black Feminine, it felt impossible to imagine the existence of a truly nurturing society, one that especially nurtured Black women. But as I have learned about Divine Mothering, I have discovered that need is a cornerstone of mothering. No matter how exhausted adults are and regardless of biological relations, a child's cry acts like a bat signal that sends them running to aid.

So, it's no surprise that anthropologists who study modern matriarchal cultures, such as the Khasi of northeastern India and the Mosuo of southwestern China, have found that they are distinctly need based. In other words, the society is organized around trying to meet everyone's needs. As scholar Heide Göttner-Abendroth is quick to point out, matriarchal societies aren't simply the reversal of patriarchal societies, with women ruling over men. Rather, they are need-based societies that are centered around the values of caretaking, nurturing, and responding to the collective needs of the community.[4] In matriarchal cultures, everyone— regardless of your gender or whether you have any biological kids—is taught to practice the societal values of caretaking, nurturing, and responding to the collective needs of the community. In such cultures, these values are the basis of what it means to be human.

Unlike whitemalegod's reign of shame, matriarchal cultures create space for us to celebrate our needs as well as our need for each other. In a need-based society, needs are valued and affirmed. And it is precisely this honoring of needs that holds the society together because needs have the power to bring us together. When I learn of a need, like a newborn's mother, my empathy is awakened, and I am motivated to help however I can. And when I am able to share vulnerably about my need, I awaken the empathy in others who then look to respond to my need. By embracing my need and the needs of others, I am invited into a relationship that is based on mutuality (rather than hierarchy) and we are able to deepen our connection because we have shared our needs.

Black women have been modeling these matriarchal values for years. For example, Black queer women's experiences of housing insecurity, rejection, isolation, and condemnation have led them to adopt the revolutionary role of "House Mothers" and reframe and expand the notion of "family." The result is an extraordinary web of interdependent, safe, affirming physical and social homes for Black queer youth. Another example is Black single mothers who, according to research conducted by social psychologist Bella DePaulo, have created such an intricate, generative web of relationships that their kids spend significantly more time with caring adults than kids of two-parent families do.[5] Two of the most vilified Black women in society are the most like Our Lady of the Sick. To the House Mother and to the Black

Single Mother: Our Lady of the Sick—the One whose heal-ing spring is always open—lives, labors, and births in you.

This is what it means to mother. No matter our gender identity, we are all invited to mother by creating life out of pain, by creating loving, interdependent community in re-sponse to violence. This is what it means to recognize that it was Our Lady of the Sick who, in the ancient book of Eze-kiel, saw an abandoned newborn choking on its own after-birth and blessed it saying, "Live! Live!"[6] She says the same to all who suffer in their need: "Live! Live! Create! Create! Relate! Relate! Live! Live! This is not the end."

Finding Her Healing Spring

When I intentionally began my journey of reconnecting my heart and head, I knew it was critical for me to connect with my need. I wanted to begin honestly, naming the pain I carried, as well as the emotions my pain elicited. But I didn't know where to begin or who could help me. Thank goodness that a friend introduced me to a matriarchal spir-itual community that could hold space for my great need. A member of the community eagerly agreed to help me process my pain, and I began by making a list of all the white men who had directly oppressed me over the course of my life. My initial list was over four hundred names long, and those were just the people I could remember. Each day, I wrote about one man on the list and the pain I still carried. Then I called my friend and shared my reflection with her. As the work continued from days to weeks to months, I finally began to recognize how much pain I carried in my young Black female body. And the rage that I had learned to silently absorb began to seep into my consciousness and overwhelm me. I felt like a ticking time bomb; for the first time in my life, I felt like I might explode.

While I was engaged in this deep healing work, I was also teaching an overwhelmingly white, theologically conservative group of university students. Many of my students were simply younger versions of the white men on my list; they were whitemalegod minions-in-the-making. In fact, in one of my "racial reconciliation" classes, I had three white male students whose actions toward me implied that my possession of a vagina disqualified me from being their professor. Every single class session, these boys sat in the front row and attempted to undermine my authority by talking over me, trying to expose me as unprepared, and firing off scripture passages that suggest that women are not to have spiritual authority over men. Every. Single. Class.

Under normal circumstances, I would have kept a tight lid on my rage. If I felt rage bubbling up, I simply gritted my teeth, trapped the rage in my mouth, and swallowed it back down. But clearly these weren't normal circumstances. In the midst of my emotional awakening, I was afraid I would lose control during class and cuss those students out—or worse!

When I shared my fear with my friend, her response stunned me.

"You might lose control, but so what? You might do something that you regret, but so what?" she questioned. Then she looked me in the eye and gently pointed her finger at me. "You get to be on a healing journey. You get to have needs. You don't have to hide your need anymore. I'm with you and I'll help you clean up any messes you think you've made."

When I heard her words, my gut exhaled. For the first time I could remember, someone was not only affirming my need, but also prioritizing my humanity over my performance. In the matriarchal way, we get to be real about our need because we are no longer alone.

Perfection is a figment of whitemalegod's imagination. It isn't real but the illusion is so powerful that I was convinced my healing journey *from whitemalegod's oppression* had to be perfect. But my friend's response invited me into the Sacred Black Feminine way; I was invited to relax into Her love, which honors our need and celebrates our imperfection. In the company of Our Lady of the Sick, I got to be real.

6

god of bulimia:
whitemalegod's war on our bodies

I learned to starve myself before I learned to read.

Many families spend Sunday morning over a bountiful brunch, but when I was five years old, my parents announced that we would no longer be allowed to eat breakfast on Sundays. Instead, we would "pray and fast for our future spouses."

I was perplexed.

Now, even with my budding cognitive skills, the abstract concept of praying and fasting for *the future* eluded my young brain because I simply couldn't comprehend a concept that had no bearing on my current physical world. My young head space was taken up with embodied activities like playing tetherball with my brother, styling my dolls' hair, and struggling through kindergarten. To my *Star Wars*–initiated brain, *the future* was in a galaxy far, far away—out of sight and beyond my known universe.

What I *could* understand was the physical pain of waking up on Sunday morning and not being allowed to sleepily pour myself a brimming bowl of Frosted Flakes. Hunger pain I understood quite well. So, as our practice of fasting got underway, I would wake up and ask, "Is today the day we starve?"

"Yes," my mom would confirm. "Today is the day we starve."

The sacrifice seemed small to my young parents who were mired in an agonizing marital bog with little practical resources to clamber their way out. They believed that if, when they were younger, they had spent more time praying and fasting for a good marriage, they could have avoided their current relational pain. Terrified that us three kids would find ourselves in a similarly painful predicament in *the future*, they taught us exactly what they had been taught: that in order to receive good things from God, like a good marriage, you must demonstrate your goodness by performing pious acts like praying and fasting. As such, every Sunday morning, my mom reminded us of the importance of fasting and praying so "God would keep us for and from our mates until the appointed time." According to her whitemalegod-derived spiritual equation, if you want to prove that you are worthy of good things—like the love and happiness of a healthy marriage—you must starve and pray and pray and starve.

As poet Nayyireh Waheed reminds us, "Mothers are humans who sometimes give birth to their pain instead of children."[1]

starving for love

Back in the good ol' days when I was in preschool, I looked forward to attending Sunday service because I excelled at memorizing Bible verses and embraced the challenge of reciting them aloud to my teacher. But under this new kindergarten-era fasting regime, the Lord's Day quickly became about coping with my hunger pain. What began as a purring pain in the morning turned into a roar by noon. Church became a torture chamber; I constantly shifted in the stiff wooden pew as I tried to get comfortable amidst my stomach's knotty rumbles and piercing aches. Despite the excruciating pain, I didn't question the fasting because it was consistent with our entire spiritual regime . . . and because I was five years old and didn't think to question what my parents or God deemed right. Indeed, unquestioned obedience to God and my parents was the only way to avoid punishment and be worthy of love. So, I submitted to the weekly starvation.

The fact that the starving was tied to love, desirability, and marriage sucked the life out of me. Though I was only five years old, I definitely understood what a spouse was. Besides the fact that Mommy and Daddy were spouses to each other, I had already learned that I should want a spouse and that I needed to be beautiful in order for a spouse to want me.

Each Sunday after church, I blew off steam by racing the boys in the church parking lot. I could sprint with the best of them, but I couldn't ever shake my biggest handicap: my tractionless patent-leather Sunday shoes. Nevertheless, the inevitable tumbles, scrapes, scabs, and budding scars seemed a small price to pay for the exhilaration of running with the wind (and boys) to my back. But one Sunday, exasperated that I continued to race and fall, Dad pivoted to fear and barked at me, "You'd better be careful. If you keep racing, you'll scar up your legs. And no man will want to marry you if you're covered in scars." The gravity in his voice shook me and I never raced again.

Though misguided, Dad was trying to protect me from pain. He instinctively knew that whitemalegod and his society graded women's bodies according to the impossible standards of white supremacy and patriarchy. Whitemalegod rules Western culture. The more a person approximates whitemalegod's whiteness and maleness, the more desirable they are perceived to be. For all the post-Civil Rights movement declarations that "Black is Beautiful," Dad knew that in whitemalegod's America, my Blackness would be a mark against my beauty, my desirability, and my value. In fact, in the Judeo-Christian scriptures darkness and Blackness are often equated with ugliness and filth. The only scripture that associates beauty with Blackness is when the Queen of Sheba says, "I am black but beautiful" (Song of Songs 1:5). But even here, Blackness is a blight, something to overcome on the path to beauty.

Dad only needed to take one glance at the Miss America pageant to know that in whitemalegod's world, Blackness is incompatible with beauty. Scholar Andrea Elizabeth Shaw points out that Black women were not even allowed to participate in the Miss America pageant until 1970, when Dad was a high school student. And I was already old enough to skin my knees at church when super light-skinned, biracial Vanessa Williams made headlines as the first Black woman to be crowned Miss America.[2] If there is ever an institution that powerfully showcases whitemalegod's society-wide choke-hold on female beauty, it is the beauty pageant world.

Really, the whole world is a Miss America pageant. Despite a woman's talent or brains, in whitemalegod's world, Dad knew that the odds were against his little Black girl, and he was scared for me. So, he scared me into submission.

It worked. Though I didn't know what *the future* was, I became convinced that starving each Sunday would ensure that, despite my scarred legs, I would be wanted. I began to believe that the prize of a spouse was worth clamoring for because having a spouse meant I was desirable. If I just starved enough to please whitemalegod, I would be beautiful, desirable, and worthy of love and the blessing of a good marriage. In this way, I implicitly learned at age five that my Black female body would only self-actualize in heterosexual marriage. By trying to protect me from harm, Dad played right into whitemalegod's hands.

Interestingly, we didn't fast and pray for anything other than marriage. By putting marriage on a pedestal, my parents taught me that my main objective in life was to please God by pleasing men. First, I was to please my dad, who enforced the fasting, and then I was to please my future husband, who was the prize for fasting. If I did all of these things perfectly, I would be loved by God, my dad, and my future husband.

I understood that I was starving for love and, like racing the boys, starving for love seemed worth it despite the immediate physical consequences.

At this point, you may be scratching your head and wondering how this belief system made sense to me and my parents. I can empathize with your conundrum. I mean, Black women are undeniably worthy and universally gorgeous. No matter our skin tone, we radiate. No matter our size, our bodies sing. No matter our hair texture, we are works of art. No matter the direction, our side-eye ushers other mortals into willing acquiescence. Our beauty is more than skin deep; it speaks of our exquisite goodness and inherent value.

So, how did we end up with a world in which well-meaning Black parents are desperately afraid that their sacred Black daughter won't be seen as good, beautiful, and worthy of any relationship she desires? And why would they resort to extreme piety and an abusive fasting regime in order to obtain a "good life" for their daughter? In order to begin to understand my parents' seemingly inexplicable behavior, we must examine how whitemalegod has used white patriarchal standards of beauty to wage a moral war on us all, especially Black women.

whitemalegod's five-hundred-year war on black female beauty

On the global stage, Black female beauty has never been fully appreciated, nor has it ever been granted the freedom to express itself on its own terms. For as long as white people and Black women have lived among one another, Black female beauty has been measured by how much it appeals to straight white men and by how much it stacks up next to white female standards of beauty. In *Fearing the Black Body: The Racial Origins of Fat Phobia*, sociologist Sabrina Strings explains that whitemalegod's society has negatively compared Black women's beauty to white women's beauty since at least the late fifteenth century, when the Black population in Europe ballooned due to the transatlantic slave trade and Black women were first incorporated into the analysis of what was considered "perfect female beauty."[3]

Immediately, Black women's bodies were measured according to the patriarchal standards of white female beauty. Though Black women's curvy and plump bodies were often considered desirable to the straight white men of the time, Black women's distinctive African facial features made them facially unattractive and thus overall less appealing than white women. Additionally, Black women's low social status as enslaved people and domestic workers fueled white men's audacity to determine Black women's beauty to be lacking relative to white women's beauty. In this way, Black women's glorious bodies were reduced to objects of white men's sexual desires and used to justify the continued oppression of Black people. Indeed, Strings writes that in fifteenth-century Antwerp, Belgium, and Venice, Italy, Black women were considered "beauties of low status and questionable facial allure but having the right proportions and just enough *embonpoint* [stoutness] to titillate European sensibilities."[4]

From the outset, Black female beauty was reduced to two things: (1) it was inferior to white female beauty, and (2) it was only acknowledged if it titillated white men. But the titillating didn't last long, for the unattainable European standards of beauty were never about human connection. Rather, they were about human domination. In such a patriarchal society, white men defined and used the standards of beauty to justify their control over all women. And in an equally white supremacist society, all white people, including white women, used the standards of beauty to justify the subjugation of Black people.

Since then, the white patriarchal system of domination has flourished, and societal perceptions of Black female beauty have remained captive to the white male gaze and shackled to negative comparisons with white women. Even as white female standards of beauty changed over the years, Black female beauty remained tethered and subjugated. For example, in seventeenth-century Europe, robustness became *the* hallmark of white female beauty. However, it wouldn't do for Black women, who were often wonderfully robust, to hit the bullseye on the standard. So, white people ignored the evidence of big Black female beauty, flipped the script, and invented a completely false narrative about Black female beauty that upheld the racial hierarchy. As Strings writes, Black women during this time were perceived as "unattractive, hypersexual, and diminutive in both size and social status." In contrast, "[Fat] white women were idealized as pure, chaste, and stately."[5] In other words, when fatness was all the rage, Black

women, regardless of their size diversity, were generally perceived as small and thus less beautiful than fat white women.
But the system of domination didn't stop there. By explicitly attaching moral behavior to perceptions of Black female
beauty, the seventeenth-century European society made it
plain: Black female beauty is inferior to white female beauty
because Black women are morally inferior to white women.
As we'll begin to see more clearly, this entire mess has whitemalegod's grubby, yet masterful, fingerprints all over it.

Indeed, when the beauty pendulum swung back in
the other direction, such as in antebellum America where
thinness was the ideal, fat phobia became yet another way
that whitemalegod maintained a system of white patriarchy.
For example, Shaw argues that the enslaved Mammy figure was used to maintain both racial and gender hierarchy
because it functioned as a physical example of what white
women should avoid embodying. Specifically, Shaw writes,
". . . [Mammy] is an inverse physiological speculum of idealized womanhood—large, dark, lumbering and yet capable,
versus being of a diminutive size, light-skinned, graceful, delicate and dependent."[6] In this deeply patriarchal American
slave society, whitemalegod left white women an alluring
trail of bread crumbs. They could enjoy and preserve their
elevated and relatively protected status as white women as
long as they remained submissive to white men and active
participants in the oppression of Black people. By supporting
and conforming to the anti-Black standards of white female
beauty, white women could accomplish both tasks in one fell
swoop. What they didn't realize was that their internalized

fat phobia didn't just keep Black women in their subjugated position; it kept white women in their place as well.

With white women duly duped and supportive of the white patriarchal system of beauty, whitemalegod turned his attention to Black people, leaving an alluring trail of bread crumbs for them too. And sadly, by the end of the Civil War, many Black people in North America had become so woefully indoctrinated by the white christ of the plantation and so violently excluded from the "life, liberty, and pursuit of happiness" that was bestowed upon white people, they were willing to do just about anything if it offered access to the "good gifts" of whiteness. Consequently, in the face of harrowing post-Reconstruction discrimination, many Black people attempted to contort themselves into whitemalegod's unattainable and anti-Black standards in the hopes of garnering safety, prosperity, and moral purity.

This impulse was cemented during the racial uplift movement, a turn-of-the-twentieth-century precursor to the civil rights movement, when many middle-class Black Americans tried to conform to white standards of respectability as a way to combat the insidious anti-Black stereotypes that threatened to destroy them. As Walker-Barnes writes, "The goal was to distance oneself from images perpetuated by stereotypes. Ironically, then, respectability, the hallmark of White, Western identity, became the hallmark of authentic Blackness."[7] As a result, many middle-class Black women raced to embody the respectability of white women and prove that they were moral and worthy humans, unlike the titillating Jezebel and the independent Mammy. But in their attempt to emulate white female respectability, Black women also readily adopted the white female ideals of thinness, which had been intertwined with morality since at least the seventeenth century. Even more, what better way to prove that one has successfully distanced oneself from impurity and the negative Jezebel and Mammy stereotypes than by garnering the approval of "respectable" white men? In this way, many Black women accepted white female beauty as the standard and opened their self-esteem to the white male gaze. In their attempt to escape white supremacy, these desperate and earnest Black women conformed to it and became imprisoned by it, thus participating in whitemalegod's shaming system of racial and gender hierarchy.

whitemalegod's beauty shame game

In the end, whitemalegod got exactly what he wanted—yet another tool to keep people trapped in shame and unable to rise up and free themselves from his clutches. For we all know female standards of beauty—and their male, trans, and non-binary counterparts—are fully unattainable. Further, social psychology research on *the halo effect* demonstrates that beauty and moral goodness are inextricably linked. When we perceive a beautiful person, we automatically deem them moral beings and even assume that they possess moral traits, such as honesty and kindness.[8] So whitemalegod has got us all in a bind. Since we can never be truly beautiful, we can never be truly good. Regardless of our gender or racial identity, this desperate but futile chase for goodness opens all of us up to a world of shame—one of whitemalegod's favorite tactics for control.

To be sure, shame is a strategic choice to hold this system of domination in balance. According to research on emotion, shame is a distinctly moral emotion. Unlike sadness, for example, shame involves feeling bad about oneself. As such, shame can powerfully influence our behavior as we seek to rid ourselves of it. However, research on motivation also teaches us that shame is an *avoidance* emotion. Unlike anger, which is an *approach* emotion that motivates people to act, shame motivates people to slink back and cower. Whitemalegod wants us to feel shame so that we invest so much mindless energy in chasing his unattainable standards of beauty and goodness that we do not rise up against his systems of domination. He wants us to feel shame so he can control us . . . forever.

That's precisely what happened to me. By the time I was born in the late twentieth century, whitemalegod had been successfully waging war on Black beauty and worth for five hundred years. My parents, much like the Black people of the racial uplift movement, instilled in me that strict adherence to whitemalegod's standards of beauty and respectability would make me worthy of good things, like marriage. And at just five years old, I was all in.

the bread of salvation

Back in my early fasting-for-my-future-spouse days, I was quickly learning that though perseverance was my forte, starving all day on Sunday was HARD. So, I was relieved to discover that Communion Sunday was my salvation. Our church celebrated the sacrament of the Eucharist once a month on the first Sunday of the month, which meant that I could legally snack during church on the first Sunday of the month. Rena, a lovely Hawaiian woman, brought a rich, buttery homemade bread for us to share during the Communion ritual. I dreamt of that lip-smacking bread all month long and when I woke up on the first Sunday of the month, my mouth was already watering for it. When it came time for me to break off a piece of bread, I grabbed the biggest chunk I could get away with and double-dunked it in the sugary grape juice. The instantaneous carbohydrate spike sent my low blood sugar soaring and I did a little hippity-hop as I returned to my seat.

But my salvation was short-lived. The sugar high ended as abruptly as it began, and I was left with even more severe hunger pains as I waited the several more hours before we returned home. Ever resourceful, I racked my brain as to how I could get access to more of that salvation bread. After a month of scheming, I decided to volunteer to help Rena with the "Communion cleanup." Ever the caring grandmother figure, I rightly calculated that once we were behind the kitchen's closed doors, Auntie Rena would invite me to "do her a favor" by finishing off the leftover Communion bread. Thus began a ritual of silencing my hunger pains by filling my little stomach with decadent bread each first Sunday of the month. Certainly, I feared that "cheating" by eating the extra bread during the fast might prevent me from earning my place in whitemalegod's graces, but in the moment, my physical desire overpowered my spiritual discipline. And over time, I discovered that the bread was good for more than just quieting my hunger pains. It also silenced my deepening fear that I would never be worthy of love. When I ate the salvation bread, love seemed bountiful and I felt safe.

One Sunday when I was in fourth grade, after Auntie Rena left me alone in the kitchen to finish the cleanup, I binged for the first time, gobbling up so much bread that I no longer felt anything—physical or spiritual. That first binge introduced me to the ecstasy of not feeling *anything*— no hunger pain, no grief, no terror, no loneliness, and no fear. I wanted to know if this was a one-time miracle or whether I could make it happen again. Though I was beginning to feel the physical nausea of an overstuffed stomach, I already had my eye on my next food target: the crystal bowl of Christmas M&Ms atop the towering bookcase in our family living room. I immediately began strategizing my next binge, at which point I hoped to be free of my constant terror.

I diligently waited until everyone—even my roomie, Des, who liked to stay up singing to herself—went to bed before I tiptoed down the dark hallway and into the living room. My mom had judiciously placed the candy bowl on the top shelf of an eight-shelf bookcase. I was too short to reach the bowl, so I used the nearby sofa as a springboard. Stretching my body as much as I could, I lunged for the bowl on the shelf. I fell woefully short and crashed to the floor, the lush carpet muffling the sound. Desperate to reach my salvation candy, I began the risky climb up the tall bookcase.

With each step up, my body clung desperately to the swaying bookcase, which was not secured to the wall. Just when I was sure the bookcase would topple and bury me in an avalanche of books, I reached the candy bowl. Hopping down onto the couch, I gobbled up the little green and red candies. As soon as I tasted the cheap sugar on my tongue, my aching loneliness vanished, and I felt like I was at a party surrounded by people who truly loved me. As I devoured several overflowing handfuls of M&Ms, I knew I would be punished if my parents discovered my illicit binge. Though it wasn't Sunday and I was allowed to eat, I was already savvy enough to leave at least some candy in the bowl so as to avoid arousing my mom's suspicion. However, in my sugar coma, I forgot to put the candy bowl back on the top shelf. But, much to my relief, no one noticed, and I was saved. And more than anything, this midnight escapade confirmed what I had hoped was true: that I could perform the miracle of making my never-ending fear go away . . . if I just got more food.

Thus, began a raging pattern of using food, especially sugar, to avoid facing my pain. I say *raging* because I learned almost immediately, and much to my horror, that nothing was going to stand in the way of me getting my food.

bulges in my body

I binged when I babysat at the neighbors' house, scavenging their freezer for cookies-'n'-cream ice cream, and then using my spoon to smooth the deep dent I had made in their half gallon carton. I binged at the summer camp buffet, relieved that no one really knew me and could tell that I was eating more than "normal." But sleepovers were my favorite place to binge because Little Caesar's pizza was abundant, bowls of buttery microwave popcorn kept magically appearing, and mini-Snickers bars were passed around the circle of girls faster than gossip. In the midst of the pampering, laughter, and '80s movie marathons, no one noticed that I did not stop eating all night. It was the one place I could binge around other people.

I was a meticulous binger, quick to cover my tracks. On the outside, everything looked dandy. I continued fasting and praying every Sunday and, since I was active in sports, I didn't gain weight. Despite the regular binges, I convinced myself and others that I was still on track to get that good life and good husband.

But I couldn't have predicted how puberty would expose my dirty little secret. Though marriage was a common topic of discussion in our family, we never spoke of sexuality, hormones, or body development. So, I was as shocked as anyone when, all of a sudden, my binges led to bulges and my once svelte body began to get pudgy in all the wrong places. Like many other girls in my fifth-grade class, I desperately wanted enough boobs to justify a coveted training bra. I didn't get the boobs, but I did get a plump stomach, chipmunk cheeks, and thick thighs.

And my parents were not happy.

Instead of telling me the universe's deepest Truth—that thick thighs save lives—they fed me more of whitemalegod's oppressive lies. In what felt like a déjà vu flashback to our conversation about my skinned knees, Dad sat me down and told me I needed to lose weight because no man would want to marry me if I was fat. Then he enlisted reinforcements to affirm his message. A few weeks later, in the privacy of his church office, my great-uncle Elmer, the family patriarch, groped my ass and told me that if it got any bigger, no man would want me. Later that year, during a public church service, a self-appointed prophet grabbed the mic, picked me out in the crowd, called me up to the front of the church, and "prophesied" that God was displeased with me because I was too fat. Whitemalegod always covers his bases, and I received the message loud and clear. I needed to do more and be better in order to be acceptable.

In this way, whitemalegod added more fiery hoops to my already hazardous spiritual obstacle course. In order to live, in order to be a human, in order to be lovable, I had to jump through even more fiery hoops. I had to fast and pray and pray and fast . . . *and lose weight.* So, I declared open war on my body.

bootcamp

My parents were eager drill sergeants in whitemalegod's war on my body. They quickly instituted new rules for me, adding a toxic exercise regimen to my already volatile relationship with food. I was not allowed breakfast until I had run around the block three times and I was not allowed to eat anything after my evening swim practice. Each night, I attempted to fall asleep amidst the pounding hunger that swimming laps for one hour will give you, only to wake up in the morning and be required to burn more calories before I "earned" the right to eat breakfast with my brother and sister.

I physically hated this new regimen but, like the Sunday morning fasting, I quickly learned to ignore my current body sensations because it meant I wouldn't miss out on a husband in the future. If anything, the new regimen of compulsory exercise and restrictions felt like a secret weapon. It was a way to contort my body into something desirable despite my binges. For I was becoming aware that my Black, bulging body was undesirable to the boys of all races in whitemalegod's world.

The exercising and restricting gave me a sense of agency in whitemalegod's world. I knew I couldn't change my Black skin, but I *could* change my weight and thus earn enough of whitemalegod's favor to get a husband. So, I committed. In fact, I so readily adopted the pattern that food is something you earn—either by fasting or exercising—that over time, I didn't need Mom and Dad to be my drill sergeants. Now that I knew what I needed to do in order to avoid gaining weight, I could be my own drill sergeant. In response to my ongoing bingeing, I just forced myself to exercise and starve.

In this way, my parents unknowingly indoctrinated me in the way of whitemalegod who only accepts and blesses you if you conform to an inhuman and unrealistic standard and somehow please the anti-Black, anti-woman whitemalegod gaze. This was an impossible feat for me; as a little Black girl, I wasn't made in his image. I could never earn whitemalegod's favor because he is incapable of loving little Black girls. But, boy, did I try!

there's no milk-and-honey in this promised land

What started as restricted eating and a little bit of extra exercise when I was in middle school turned into a full-blown eating disorder and extreme body dysmorphia by high school. When I was fifteen, I left my middle-class, racially diverse public high school in California and transferred to Phillips Exeter Academy, an extremely white, elite boarding school in New Hampshire. Way back in 1781, whitemalegod founded Exeter as a training ground for his ever-expanding brood of white patriarchal minions, such as Facebook CEO Mark Zuckerberg, novelist Dan Brown, and US President Franklin Pierce.

On the one hand, I was thrilled to be at Exeter because, at my core, I'm a nerd and I was bored out of my mind in my public school honors classes. At Exeter, I finally encountered a rigorous intellectual environment that made my mind-heart sing! But on the other hand, as a Black girl on financial aid, I was accosted by a level of community marginalization that was new even to me. In this unfamiliar white world of lacrosse and hockey jocks, summer houses in the Hamptons, private helicopters, and famous parents, I was surrounded by whitemalegod's gaze.

An all-boys school for the first two hundred years of its existence, white patriarchy continued to rule Exeter's student body while I was there. Though all the students were extraordinarily talented and bright, our social value as female students seemed based on whether the rich white boys were attracted to us. Sure, it was cool to be a genius on the violin, an All-American softball player, or a math prodigy. But at the end of the day, it wasn't our abundant talents that mattered. Our perceived attractiveness, according to the pubescent white male sons of powerful white men like Donald Trump, determined our value. I was a contestant in the Miss America pageant for the Ivy League–bound.

As a transfer student in an insular boarding-school community, I carried the burden of acclimating to an alien world while also tripping over my shame about my Black female body. Intoxicated by my shame and unaware that the pageant was rigged, I became obsessed with fitting in to a community that was inherently incapable of valuing my Black femaleness. Much like when I was at home, I sought validation outside myself. But this time, the holders of my external validation were not my Dad or the Black and brown boys from my church youth group. They were the rich white boys of America's most exclusive high school. For the first time in my life, whitemalegod's gaze was explicitly and undeniably white. Though I excelled academically and in sports, I was convinced that in order to survive this elite world, I needed to solicit whitemalegod's gaze among the very "princes of Maine and kings of New England" that fellow Exeter alum John Irving extols in *The Cider House Rules*.

In all honesty, the whitemalegod gaze I encountered at Exeter wasn't all that different from what I had encountered in my own Black home. At home, I had learned that the more people approximated white patriarchal standards of beauty—for example, a skeletal body size, lighter skin tone, and chemically straightened hair—the more affirmation they would receive from Dad. The standards were the same at Exeter, but this time they were enforced by an army of rich white boys. I wish I had been one of the Black girls who just didn't give a fuck what those rich white boys thought. But I absolutely gave a fuck because I knew that in order to be a valuable woman and worthy of God's gift of good marriage, I needed to be desirable to the men around me.

Many of the rich white boys at Exeter were enamored by the Black girls. (How could they not? We were fabulous. Every. Single. One. Of. Us.) But the rich white boys couldn't actually admit to being smitten with us because our Black girlhood existed entirely outside of whitemalegod's tiny, terrifying circle of acceptability. Though the rich white boys repeatedly told me that I was "pretty for a Black girl," it wasn't socially acceptable to actually date a Black girl. So, the rich white boys would creep up on us under cover of darkness and attempt to hook up with us (with varied levels of success). But then, the following day, during broad daylight while surrounded by their lacrosse bros, they would pretend they didn't know us.

Just like whitemalegod and the fifteenth-century, straight white men of Antwerp and Venice, the rich white boys tolerated us as long as we met their physical needs and didn't compromise their position in the white patriarchal pecking order. At best, we were assets, tossed away when we were no longer valuable to them. At worst, we were enslaved Black women on a bizarre New England plantation. This experience of exploitation was so common among the Black girls that we mockingly created a name—the BG Club, short for the Black Girl Club—to describe this horrifying group of rich white boys. We even identified the worst predators and named them the president, vice president, secretary, and treasurer of the BG Club. We laughingly tossed about the BG Club name in order to avoid crying about the reality that these rich white boys treated us worse than they would one day treat their mistresses. I hid my pain by giggling along. But I secretly made plans to attempt the impossible: achieve legitimacy among these princes of Maine and kings of New England.

Since I'd been battling my body, silencing myself, and taking cues from white patriarchal culture my entire life, I knew exactly what I needed to do. Under the pious guise of fasting, I began starving myself every Wednesday and also for three straight days during the first weekend of each month. For those seven days per month, I drank lots of water but consumed zero food. The rest of the month, I fastidiously only ate honeydew melon, plain bagels, and low-fat cottage cheese with the occasional binge on fat-free pretzels now and then.

In order to achieve the skeletal body I craved, I also added extra exercise to my daily schedule. Though I was a three-season varsity athlete with grueling daily practices, I did an extra hour of cardio in the gym after practice each day. My hair was falling out in clumps, my eyelids were constantly twitching, and I suffered from regular fainting spells. But I was the thinnest I had ever been. When I returned home for my first break, my dad greeted me with a bear hug and said, "There's the beautiful girl I always knew was in there!"

Dad's gaze seemed perfectly in line with the whitemale-god gaze at Exeter. The more Dad was enthralled with my beauty, the more the rich white boys seemed to be enthralled too. Now a limber size 4, the rich white boys began noticing me. Within weeks, I had my first real boyfriend—a rich white boy who seemed honored to be seen in public with me. And perhaps more importantly, Dad was paying attention to me. Though he had rarely attended my sports events when I attended public school in my hometown, he flew all the way across the country to attend my basketball game against our rival Andover. Just months later, he flew back to Exeter to take me prom dress shopping (because I was going to prom! With a boy! Which meant maybe someone *would* want to marry me! Woot woot!). Now that I was beautiful, I was worthy of Dad's attention and whitemalegod's good gift of marriage. I was something special.

trapped

I was immediately hooked on this new designer drug: my dad's and, by proxy, whitemalegod's love. I decided to do anything and everything to chase the high.

That didn't go well.

From my teens to my thirties I was trapped in a cycle of restricting, bingeing, and compulsive exercising—first as an undergraduate at whitemalegod's Dartmouth College and then at whitemalegod's predominantly white Santa Barbara, California, where I earned my PhD. No matter my size, I was never satisfied with my weight nor fully embraced by the white communities that surrounded me. Without contemporary social media jewels like Black Twitter, I was perpetually trapped in predominantly white worlds without any input that was untainted by whitemalegod's anti-Black, anti-woman gaze. I remained so preoccupied with my size that, despite my twelve-hour work days in my doctoral psychology lab, I held memberships at two different gyms so I could work out at one gym each morning and work out at the other gym each evening without anyone noticing my unhealthy obsession with exercise. I starved myself regularly, sometimes for weeks at a time, in order to fit into a dress for an important fundraiser or to prepare for summer bikini weather, but I called it fasting because, by that point, I could no longer distinguish between the two. If Black Twitter had been around then, perhaps a Black Auntie would have told me that the best way to have a beach body is to take your actual body to the beach. But the only voice I ever heard was whitemalegod's, which declared that my Black female body would never be beachworthy.

Though I continuously binged, as I moved into my late twenties, my discipline began to weaken, and I couldn't always muster up the discipline to restrict and overexercise to compensate for the increasingly common binges. This led to a brutal cycle of extreme weight gain and loss, a closet full of clothes ranging from size 4 to 18, and—most debilitating of all—distorted beliefs about my weight, appearance, and value that tormented me. I was never enough—never beautiful, never valuable, never *somebody*. Often during my public-facing career, I was more concerned with how my thighs looked on the Jumbotron than with connecting with the audience. I was deeply ashamed of my struggle and I didn't believe I could be honest about it. The shame always sent me deeper into food.

The fact that I remained unmarried throughout my twenties and on into my thirties while all of my close (white) friends married seemed to only confirm that whitemalegod wasn't pleased with me and that I was unlovable. Indeed, that I was unlovable was the belief I internalized the most. It seemed to define my existence and my reality; it was the truest thing about me. Thirty years after I first began fasting with the goal of one day becoming worthy of love, I was still chasing after whitemalegod's elusive love.

7

She Whose Thick Thighs Save Lives

I learned that getting married wasn't my most pressing issue right around the time that George Zimmerman was acquitted of the murder of Trayvon Martin. Like many other Black millennials, my racial consciousness skyrocketed in response to the 2013 acquittal of a white man who killed a Black boy. As we watched how white America, particularly law enforcement, rabidly defended Zimmerman, Black people in my generation were violently forced to recognize that America was no safer for us than it was for our parents and grandparents. Fear invaded my Black female body because I lived right next door to the police precinct in an overpoliced, predominantly Black, Minneapolis neighborhood. Not surprisingly, the goal of getting married was immediately eclipsed by the goals of simply staying alive and working to protect all Black lives. Overwhelmed by the horror that my unlovableness was systemic rather than individual, I jumped into action. Without pausing to tend to my own pain, I wrote op-eds, I marched, I led antiracism trainings, I lectured to large audiences on nonconscious bias, and I argued with white liberals on social media. Within a year, I was burnt out and bingeing more than ever to numb my terror. I was bingeing so late into the night that I couldn't keep my food stocked. Even though I lived alone, I ended up getting a Costco membership so I could keep enough food in the house to feed my binges while minimizing my trips to the grocery store. Each week, I gobbled down a bulk-sized bin of Jelly Bellys because the sugar artificially elevated my mood and energy level and, for a fleeting moment, eased my existential terror.

As a frontline activist and scholar, I experienced constant terror that led me to compulsively eat. For example, in the wake of white police officer Darren Wilson's nonindictment for the murder of unarmed Black teen Mike Brown, my university students and I participated in the now-iconic Black Lives Matter demonstration that ultimately shut down America's largest mall on the Saturday before Christmas 2014, the busiest shopping day of the year.[1] Surrounded by a jovial crowd of marchers amidst the backdrop of cheery Christmas tunes and festive decorations, I was initially overjoyed to participate in the large gathering calling for the end of anti-Black police brutality. Together we sang, chanted, and proclaimed the dignity of Black people. But as the crowd grew larger and our collective voice grew more powerful, it became more difficult for shoppers to get around us and into the stores. Whatever hospitality the Mall of America officials had extended to us abruptly ended as soon as we began to disrupt capitalism—one of whitemalegod's prized drugs.

Within minutes, the mall officials antagonized us, turning a powerful affirmation of Black life into a dystopian nightmare. The police were called in, and they violently showed up in full riot gear. As the police encircled us, the mall intercom repeatedly played a creepy, robotic message threatening us to disperse in order to avoid arrest. Nevertheless, we continued singing and chanting. I pulled my students in closer to me in an attempt to comfort them and to increase the distance between us and the Stormtrooper police.

As we stood our ground, the situation escalated. The intercom message began issuing "final warnings" and the Stormtroopers began moving in toward the crowd and forcefully arresting people. As the crowd of several thousand began to panic, I was triggered with fear. Whitemalegod's use of force to squelch our demonstration for Black dignity triggered all the trauma I unknowingly carried about my own indignity as a Black woman, and a wave of fear coursed through my body. As I frantically looked around, all I saw were Stormtroopers. There were so many of them and we were completely surrounded. For some reason, I could no longer hear the Christmas music; I could only hear the dystopian voice threatening us. I stopped breathing, my spine trembled, and my gut formed a knot so fierce that my torso began to experience piercing cramps. The fear gripped the loudspeaker in my body, and I couldn't hear Love anymore.

Many arrests were made that day, but my students and I managed to escape. The clanging waves of fear never stopped, however, even after I returned to my home. And unlike the

Love waves, these fear waves *hurt*. My body wouldn't stop shaking. I couldn't make the fateful thoughts that Black lives will never matter go away, and the cramps were relentless. In the midst of overwhelming trauma and fear, I couldn't find my way back to the Love that is, somehow, beneath it all. Having only experienced it once at the daylong mindfulness retreat the month before, I didn't yet have a reliable practice for connecting with Love. I did, on the other hand, have a reliable practice for silencing the fear. I ate every last thing in my well-stocked kitchen and then stumbled to bed.

The urge to vomit awakened me abruptly. As I involuntarily puked up the cans of olives, hunks of cheap cheddar cheese, and cartons of milk I deliriously devoured the night before, I longed for freedom from bingeing. But I knew of no other way to deal with life. Further, I had no idea that my bingeing was tied to my terror. The excruciating terror-binge cycle continued, with each month more hopeless than the previous one. My whole life, I had thought binging was about controlling my body in order to be desirable, worthy of love. But as my mindfulness meditation practice deepened, I began to connect the dots that bingeing was my lifelong go-to for fear management.

After another appalling episode of post-justice work bingeing, I had a mindful *Aha!* moment.

"That's interesting," I said to myself in the dark. "Whether it is the fear that no one will ever marry me or the fear of anti-Black police brutality, I compulsively turn to food."

After three gruesome decades of bingeing, fasting, and excessive exercise, my mindfulness practice uncovered a cause-and-effect relationship. Clutching my still-throbbing stomach with one hand, I used my other hand to peck out a desperate, middle-of-the-night google search on compulsive eating and spirituality. The first search result was an upcoming "food and spirituality" retreat only twenty miles from my house. So, I grabbed my credit card and registered.

At the retreat, I heard countless personal stories from people who, just like me, had experienced horrors with food and body image, but, unlike me, they had found healing. Surrounded by those surprisingly familiar strangers, I felt safe enough for the first time to express the self-love that powers three revolutionary words: "I need help."

I related to all the stories, but one young woman's story stood out. As Elsa shared her harrowing story of childhood trauma, compulsive overeating, and body dysmorphia, I leaned in. Despite all that had happened to her, Elsa carried a Peace that reminded me of the Love waves I had recently encountered at the mindfulness retreat. As Elsa spoke, she stood tall with dignity and strength, like she was planted in Love. She embodied a formidable force, but not the kind that abused. Though Elsa's story resonated with me, I was even more drawn to her palpable emotional health. Like the Love waves, I didn't understand it, but I wanted to surrender to it. Plus, she was wearing the most fabulous pair of black suede thigh-high boots I had ever seen.

After she spoke, I approached her and impulsively blurted out, "Whatever it is you have, I want it."

She said, "You absolutely can have it. You have everything you need to heal. It's already in you. You just have to find it." Elsa invited me to her compulsive food–behavior recovery program, and I attended my first meeting with her the following day.

I jumped into the recovery program with gusto. I worked with a nutritionist to identify a personalized food plan that would provide the nutrients and energy my body needed, I limited my aerobic exercise to only thirty minutes a day, and I stopped eating sugar.

On the upside, following my food and exercise plan was easy. I was amazed at how quickly the compulsion to eat and over-exercise melted away once I had a specific plan to follow. On the downside, dealing with reality without compulsive eating and exercise to numb my pain was excruciating. During the first week on my food and exercise plan, I traveled to Geneva, Switzerland, to give a series of social science lectures on justice and Black dignity. For the first time in my career, I had to talk publicly about racial injustice without food and exercise, my drugs of choice, to get me through it. After I completed my lectures, which essentially implored the mostly non-Black audience of global leaders to give a shit about Black people, I returned to my hotel and realized for the first time that this is what I do for a living: try to persuade white people to care about me. My entire career was built on the dehumanizing practice of whimsically and eloquently presenting an argument for my humanity in the hopes that people under the spell of whitemalegod would maybe one day hopefully possibly potentially wake up and give a shit.

One week without compulsive eating and exercise and I was already uncovering some of the layers of dehumanization inherent in my work. Somewhere along the line, I had been taught that in order to be human, I needed to convince white people that I'm human. Somewhere along the line, I had been taught that in order to accomplish justice, I needed to convince white people that I am worthy of justice. Somewhere along the line, I had been taught that justice can only be accomplished if white people are involved. Somewhere along the line, I had been taught that it was my work to convince white people to affirm my humanity. In many ways, I was already aware of the collective pain that Black people experience, but my moment of reckoning in that Swiss hotel room awakened me to the truth that I had been centering white people even as I claimed to work for the liberation of Black people. (Unbeknownst to me, whitemalegod was still the center of my moral universe, so of course his minions were the center of my justice universe.)

Beyond centering white people, I also awakened to the anti-Blackness I experienced in my justice work. Though I had been heralded as a "trailblazer" in the mostly white, male-dominated Christian world, my justice work had extracted me from the safe spaces that nurture and protect me as a Black woman and catapulted me into the unsafe and oppressive spaces of the powerful where I was exposed to the soul-crushing forces of its institutional racism, sexism, and poisonous theology. In those spaces, I gave much yet received little more than lip service and a steady stream of macroaggressions.

As these horrors dominated my conscious awareness, a wildfire of rage rose within me and my house-of-cards career began to incinerate. Without compulsive eating and exercise to extinguish the roaring flames, I needed a Protector and a Balm. This sounded like a job for the Sacred Black Feminine.

Encountering She Whose Thick Thighs Save Lives

I was completely new to the recovery world, so I didn't know that spirituality lies at the heart of many recovery programs, including mine. At one meeting, a woman shared that the program not only helps us get free from unhealthy food behaviors, it also helps us develop a spirituality that works under all conditions. When I heard this, my spine straightened, and I leaned forward in my seat. A spirituality that works under all conditions? Even in the midst of ongoing Black genocide and persistent feelings of undesirability? If this was true, I wanted to learn more about this spirituality.

As I talked to different members of the program and read some of the literature, I discovered that we were each encouraged to identify and clearly describe a Higher Power that was trustworthy, unconditionally loving, and fueled the hope we needed to face life without food to numb us. As we deepened our relationship with this Higher Power and surrendered our food behaviors to Them, we would begin to experience a spirituality that works even when life is full of pain. As I learned more about this, my soul bubbled up with liberating hope! As someone who had spent years in constrictive religious circles, I had never encountered a spiritual

Our Lady of the Good Death who helps us die to our false selves and promises that death yields restorative goodness (Clermont-Ferrand, France; twelfth century).

The Black Virgin of Moulins to whom Joan of Arc prayed in 1429. If Harriet Tubman had prayed before a Black Madonna statue, I bet it would've been this one (France; eleventh century).

She Who Cherishes Our Hot Mess—and pieces us back together. She is officially known as Our Lady of the Sick (Vichy, France; fourteenth century).

She Whose Thick Thighs Saves Lives declares, "I am Black and I am beautiful." She is officially known as Our Lady of the Fountain because the best water in town flowed from Her loins (Mende, France; age unknown).

The Virgin-Warrior is the God of Consent who redefines what it means to be pure and loves by letting go (Thuret, France; seventeenth-century replacement of the thirteenth-century original).

The Black Virgin of Saint-Gervazy helps us find our way home (France; twelfth century).

No matter where we are on our journey, the Mother of All Bling is among us, just waiting to shower Her sacred lavishness on us. She is also known as the Black Virgin of La-Chapelle-Geneste (France; sixteenth-century copy of an older version).

"She is Black because She is Black." Our Lady of the Side-Eye, also known as Our Lady of the Rock, is unapologetically Black and unapologetically pro-Black (Mayres, France; twelfth century).

group that actually cheered me on as I defined God in a way that resonated with me and forged my own unique path to the divine. Though I was already journeying toward the Sacred Black Feminine, the encouragement to clearly and specifically describe my Higher Power opened up space for me to blatantly express what I needed in a Higher Power.

First, I began by blatantly expressing what I *didn't* need in a Higher Power, especially one to whom I was going to surrender my food behaviors. What I didn't need was anything that resembled the whitemalegod that I had been taught to see as my Higher Power. Even though I had grown up in whitemalegod's world, it wasn't until that moment that I realized that I really, really, really hated *Him*. The Him whose fiery hoops I've been jumping through my whole life. The Him who told me that no one would want to marry me if I was fat. The Him who would only give me good things if I contorted myself into some*thing* that pleased his whitemalegod gaze. The Him who got me into this mess. No, I wasn't going to be turning my will and life over to Him. In order to get the help I needed to heal my relationship to food and body, I needed to trust in a Higher Power who truly had my back. Whitemalegod wouldn't do and neither would some fake-ass white ally god named Karen.

If I was going to ask for help and truly surrender my life, I needed a Higher Power that was a true miracle worker, a Higher Power I could trust to lovingly get the job done. I generally knew Her as the Sacred Black Feminine, but the recovery program encouraged me to be more specific about my needs. In order to experience a spirituality that worked under all the conditions of my life as a Black woman, I needed to get clear about exactly what I needed in a Higher Power and begin to believe I was worthy of such a Higher Power.

One morning before dawn, I decided to try describing this Higher Power. I began tentatively, unsure that it was actually legal to do this. After years of constrictive religious conditioning, I hadn't yet internalized what Black trans spiritual teacher Marty S. invites us all to believe, "I have a right to a relationship with the divine that is self-defined and self-guided."[2] But as I recalled the mystical waves of Love that pinned me down at the mindfulness meditation retreat years before, goosebumps popped up all over my arms urging me to call out my needs.

So, I started slowly, pip-squeaking out an almost imperceptible declaration:

I am worthy of a Higher Power who loves my Blackness.

I cleared my throat and repeated myself because I was trying to convince myself of this truth.

I am worthy of a Higher Power who loves my Blackness.

The second time's the charm. Now I was on a roll.

I am worthy of a Higher Power who listens to, values, and validates my experiences as a Black woman.

I am worthy of a Higher Power who is fiercely nurturing.

I am worthy of a Higher Power who is engaging and relatable.

I am worthy of a Higher Power who is a giver of joy!

I am worthy of a Higher Power who demands nothing from me, yet freely offers every spiritual treasure to me.

I am worthy of a Higher Power who embraces my emotions no matter how loud they are.

I am worthy of a Higher Power who honors my process no matter how messy it may seem.

I am worthy of a Higher Power who loves all my body sizes.

I am worthy of a Higher Power who rejoices in my imperfection.

With each affirmation, my holy audacity grew, emboldening my declaration of what I demanded in a Higher Power. The spiritual space around me magically deepened and widened, making more space for me to work—as if it knew that this encounter with my true Higher Power would have me boldly taking up space in whitemalegod's world. As the space expanded, so did I, and I became even more specific in my demands.

I am worthy of a Higher Power who does not just listen *to my experiences as a Black woman, She* understands *my experiences as a Black woman.*

I am worthy of a Higher Power who knows the pain I face on a daily basis as a Black woman.

I am worthy of a Higher Power who stands beside me at the fatal intersection of white supremacy and patriarchy.

I am worthy of a Higher Power who exists in a body that is also scorned by the society.

I am worthy of a Higher Power who is *a Black woman.*

Making Peace with My Body

This epic process of rejecting the Higher Power I *should* have and instead freely choosing the Higher Power I *needed* helped me to unlearn a whitemalegod lie that had tormented me my entire life. The belief that *the source of my validation exists outside of me* had sent me begging for validation from Dad, random guys, and even a supposedly unconditionally loving God. But once I specified my own Higher Power, I realized I could choose *anything* because I don't need other people to validate my choices. I could validate my own choices, just like I validated my description of the Sacred Black Feminine.

I could choose what I believe rather than simply accepting what I had been taught. I could choose who I want to be in relationship with rather than remaining in relationships out of obligation. I could choose to adopt the term *Deeper Power* rather than *Higher Power* because it powerfully rejects patriarchal and hierarchical thinking and relating to the Divine. And I could choose how I feel about my body rather than letting whitemalegod's media tell me.

The Sacred Black Feminine helped me embrace my own free will in all these aspects but She especially helped me choose to embrace my body despite what society said about it. As I began to turn to images of the Black Madonna to guide me, I noticed they are not small women. They look like they have never fasted a day in their life. They look like they eat more than my boarding school staples of plain bagels, honeydew melon, and nonfat cottage cheese. They proudly take up space. And there's a seriousness to the way in which they hold themselves, as if they really can't be bothered by what whitemalegod thinks of their bodies. They have actual work to do.

The four-hundred-fifty-plus Black Madonnas around the world encompass a wide range of skin colors, hair textures, body sizes, and ages. Some are pregnant. Some are breastfeeding with proudly exposed breasts. Some are gender nonconforming. The one thing they all have in common is that they are Black and they are holy. Seeing these diverse liberating images of the Sacred Black Feminine helped me relax into my body because I was able to relax into Her diverse and inclusive body. The opposite of whitemalegod's non-body, Her body is infinitely relatable and always expanding to include Her precious children. There is enough room for all of us. We can all find ourselves in Her body. We can all relax into Her body.

As I continued to surrender to Her healing body, I began to realize that, despite what whitemalegod had taught me, my body was not an enemy to be subdued and colonized. I began to let go of an ideal body size and instead slowly built peace with my body. I began each day by getting out of the shower, compassionately examining my naked body in the full-length mirror, and reminding myself that my body was my best friend. Unlike whitemalegod, my body had never rejected me, given up on me, starved me, broken up with me, or threatened me. Despite all that whitemalegod had done to it, my body was still doing its absolute best to keep me alive. I cultivated compassion for my body by each day focusing on one part of my body and verbally thanking it for being on my side and working to keep me alive, despite it all.

After months of practicing daily body gratitude, I experienced a magical shift. One day, I looked in the mirror and realized that my body was the physical representation of the Sacred Black Feminine. Through all my issues with bingeing, restricting, and over-exercising, She had been with me all along—affirming, sustaining, and supporting me—in the form of my body. Through all of my failed attempts to win validation from whitemalegod and his minions, She had been there all along, keeping me alive and sticking by my side. Shocked and still naked, I dropped to the hardwood floor and instinctively stretched my arm toward my reflection in the mirror. I wanted to touch Her holy and beautiful body. I wanted to touch my holy and beautiful body.

I experienced a second miracle months later as I walked more than four hundred miles across central France to visit ancient Black Madonnas in remote mountain villages. In the past, my obsession with being a waif and my compulsion to over-exercise would have gone on overdrive at the thought of *walking* four hundred miles. But my first thought after making the decision to walk the pilgrimage wasn't "Yay! I can't wait to see how much weight I'm going to lose on this 'spiritual pilgrimage.' I'm going to be so beautiful and thin by the end." Rather, my first thought was "I need to check in with my nutritionist to see how much extra food I'll need in order to be healthy and present for this epic spiritual journey."

The thought surprised me because I had never prioritized being healthy and present over being thin, and I knew that this meant that I was healing. I was becoming more and more one with Her body. When I walked up to Her altar on my pilgrimage, I wanted to be just as unbothered as She was.

Fuck Off, You Princes of Maine, You Kings of New England

Storm clouds boomed as I traversed the two-lane country road on my way to Mende, an eighteen-hundred-year-old city in southern France on my way to visit Our Lady of the Fountain. I was riding shotgun in a Smart car–sized blue car, and I was at the mercy of a chain smoking, Evel Knievel–wannabe I had met via a rideshare app. Mende was way outside my walking radius, but I was eager to see the *two* Black Madonnas that coreigned the city. Louis, my "driver," was supposedly making the two-hour trip to Mende in order to visit his grandmother, but the eighteen-year-old newly licensed driver hugged the tight curves like he was trying to win a video game rather than survive the snaking, slick road.

With one hand clutching an unfiltered cigarette and another hand sort of guiding the steering wheel, he simultaneously polluted the cramped car and maniacally accelerated before each sharp turn. Grateful that the looming rain hadn't yet begun, I rolled down the passenger window, leaned my head out, and drank up the damp, fresh air. As we barreled toward a curve, Louis temporarily released his grip on the steering wheel so he could turn up the already-blaring radio. I clutched the handlebar just above the window, as if that would save me from Louis the Daredevil. If I had known how incredible my encounter with the Black Madonnas of Mende would be, I would have prayed to them for safety and protection.

After a dozen scares, Louis and I pulled up to the main square outside the cathedral just as the rain began to fall. I had barely grabbed my backpack from the backseat, when Louis abruptly shifted into first gear and roared away. I yelled, "Merci," and looked up at the clouds. I could handle a bit of rain but the rumbling, slate-colored sky suggested it was going to rain long and hard.

One of the Black Madonnas, Our Lady of the Fountain, lived outside, so I decided to visit Her first before the storm descended. As I made my way through the mazelike, pedestrian-only city center, the cobblestone streets began to darken with rain. I wasn't exactly sure where Our Lady of the Fountain lived and there were decoys on almost every corner. The people of Mende are so devoted to their Black Madonnas that many of them have built elaborate, sturdy shrines on the exterior walls of their medieval homes. So, as I walked the ancient Roman city center looking for the actual Lady of the Fountain, I encountered dozens of gorgeous ministatues of Her. Since many of the old Black Madonnas do not conform to whitemalegod's "bigger is better" philosophy, they are actually pretty small in size and easy to overlook. Despite the continuous rain, I prudently stopped to examine and appreciate each shrine just so I didn't miss Her.

But as the storm brewed, I began to get desperate. On a sunny day, I would have loved savoring each shrine. But it was raining and, epic pilgrimage or not, I'm just another Black woman who doesn't want to get her hair wet.

"Where is She?" I asked aloud in the empty, stormy street.

Just then, I turned a corner and spotted another smallish Black Madonna enclosed in a simple glass case at the opposite end of a spacious courtyard. At first, I thought it was another copy but when I saw a small sign proclaiming Her name in French, *Notre Dame des Fontaines*, I knew I had found Her.

As I approached Her in the drizzle, I saw that She was incredibly weathered. Most of her facial features were dulled, parts of Her body had chipped away, and She was covered in a grimy patina. But as I stood before Her, I marveled. Though She wasn't the oldest Black Madonna I visited, She was by far the most battered—and Her ancient tattered body called into question whether Her Black life mattered. Yet Her stout body stood tall, firmly hoisted by Her thick thighs. Clearly, She wasn't going anywhere.

As I stepped back to examine Her in the context of Her surroundings, I noticed that a massive white male angel towered above Her carrying a vast banner. The banner read *Nigra sum sed formosa* the ancient Judeo-Christian text from the Song of Songs that means "I am Black but I am beautiful."

I had discovered in my research that *Nigra sum sed formosa* was a racist slur. I knew it was a deliberate slavery-era mistranslation of the original Hebrew designed to denigrate Black people by separating Blackness from beauty. I knew that the correct biblical translation was *Nigra sum* et *formosa*, which means "I am Black *and* I am beautiful" (*italics* mine). So, I gasped when I saw that for centuries a white male angel has perpetually hoisted this slur over Her beautiful, battered Black body.

"You too?" I cried. "They told you your Blackness was an impediment to your beauty too?"

As I gazed at the banner above Her, I recalled all of the times the prep-school boys told me "Wow, you're pretty . . .

for a Black girl" and my tears began to mingle with the falling rain.

"You were taught to be at war with your Black body too? You were taught to question whether your Black body matters too? Your Black body has been living and breathing and fighting under this horrible anti-Black banner for centuries?"

I felt Her pain and reached out to embrace Her but was stopped by the glass case surrounding Her. So, I instinctively cradled my own body because it seemed that our bodies were one. Her story was my story. Her burden of anti-Blackness was my burden. Her body was my body.

Just then, the sky stopped restraining itself and torrential rain began to fall. I knew She was weeping with me.

As I held us both, I gazed deeply at Her face. She held Her hefty cheeks high, just as Her stout body stood firmly tall. Defiance covered Her face, as if She knew about the centuries-old slur above Her and simply wasn't going to succumb to its meaning. The peaceful resistance in Her eyes told a story that powerfully overrode the ancient anti-Black message in the banner above Her.

Her eyes said:

I am Black and I am beautiful. I don't care what the Bible translation says about me.

I am Black and I am beautiful. I don't care what the Renaissance artists painted over me.

I am Black and I am beautiful. I don't care what the white male angels are saying.

I am Black and I am beautiful. I don't care how long the princes and kings of the day chant slurs at me.

I am Black and I am beautiful.

Periodt.

As my gaze followed the length of Her beautiful Black body, I noticed that just beneath Her thick thighs stood an antique water spigot. When I saw the water source, I was reminded that She was called Our Lady of the Fountain. According to legend, She possesses this title because Her fountain provided the best water in town, the kind of water that literally saves lives in a medieval world full of disease, limited medical care, and jaw-dropping inequality.

Facing Her head-on, I knew I could bring all of my Black female body to Her. Though She empathizes with my pain as a Black woman, She stands proudly and beautifully, Her thick thighs offering life-saving waters that tell a different story: I am Black and I am beautiful. Emboldened by Her, I began to repeat the liberating messages that emanated from Her defiant eyes.

"I am Black and I am beautiful," I said to Her.

"I am Black and I am beautiful," I repeated louder, and to no one in particular.

Our Black bodies still merged, I shared in Her boldness. My stance widened and I pulled my chin up.

"I am Black and I am beautiful," I screamed, out-roaring the storm.

Amidst the unrelenting downpour, I soaked up Her life-saving water and continued my freedom chant.

I am Black and I am beautiful. I don't care what the Bible translation says about me.

I am Black and I am beautiful. I don't care what society's banners are saying about me.

I am Black and I am beautiful. I don't care how long you say "all lives matter" to me.

I am Black and I am beautiful. I don't care what the prep-school boys told me.

I am Black and I am beautiful. So, fuck off, you Princes of Maine, you Kings of New England!

I am Black and I am beautiful.

Periodt.

8

machiavellian monster:
whitemalegod's liturgy of fear

When I was six years old, I learned what happens to women who make their own choices. Toward the end of what seemed like a typical Sunday morning church service, a commotion erupted on the far left of the vast stage. I watched with curiosity as several men escorted a reluctant young white woman past the orchestra pit, by the one-hundred-person mass choir, and up to the front and center of the stage where both the commanding pulpit and her white father—our pastor—awaited her. Once the woman had been safely delivered to her father, the male escorts retreated.

I had recently attended my first wedding and had been enticed by the rice shower, abundant flowers, and expectant joy. Thinking this was another wedding, I silently clapped my hands in glee. But within moments, I realized that this was not a festive occasion. I couldn't see the woman's face because her head hung low, her chin grazing her chest. Nevertheless,

I knew something was terribly wrong. Shame, rather than a bridal veil, covered her face.

Within moments, the father-pastor nervously grabbed the microphone and said, "I have an announcement to make."

My curiosity piqued, I leaned forward in the pew.

"My daughter is pregnant and, as you all know, she is not married. As a father, I have failed to raise a virtuous daughter. And as your pastor, I have failed you all. If a man can't lead his own family, how can he lead a congregation? For this reason, I have offered my resignation to the board of elders."

The woman stared at the plush, royal blue carpet. She was not offered a chance to speak.

I looked at the young woman's lowered head and felt roaring waves of fear crush my body. Even though no physical violence occurred that morning, I looked at the woman and instinctively understood that she was receiving a public beating.

I didn't really know how babies were made, but I had both a mommy and a daddy, so I figured babymaking somehow involved a daddy too. But the daddy was nowhere in sight. The young woman stood alone in her shame, in front of thousands of congregants who now had knowledge of her most intimate behaviors. That seemed cruel to me, and as I witnessed it, I reflexively clinched and curled my body into a defensive posture. I felt unsafe in the church—the very place I was supposed to feel most safe.

I looked to my parents, who were seated next to me, for assurance. But they simply nodded their heads in approval of the beating. I look around me and noticed that the other congregants seemed to approve as well. Afraid to show my fear and confusion, I remained silent and clung to the pew cushion like it was a baby blanket—a soft comfort in the midst of terror.

Later, we lunched with a fellow congregant who was also a physician. When my mother commented on the events of the service and the young woman's pregnancy, the doctor couldn't resist sharing a bit of juicy gossip. You see, the father-pastor had asked the doctor to "examine" the young woman. During the examination, the gossip-doctor discovered that the young woman's hymen was still fully intact, concluding that she had not actually been penetrated. When the gossip-doctor and the father-pastor interrogated the young woman, she admitted that she had been "fooling around" with her boyfriend and that they hadn't engaged in penile-vaginal intercourse. The gossip-doctor was more than happy to regale us with both his juicy tidbit as well as his expert medical opinion: "I guess there was just semen flying around and some of it got inside her and impregnated her."

I didn't know what a hymen was or what being penetrated involved or even what semen was, but I had successfully completed stranger-danger training at kindergarten, where I had learned that I had private parts that I didn't have to share with anyone, ever. So, I couldn't understand why the young woman had to share her private parts with the doctor. And I wasn't sure why we were talking about the young woman's private parts while munching on chicken salad sandwiches.

I was so confused. But my mom cleared it up for me.

"You see," my mom murmured. "She didn't even have real sex and she got pregnant. You can't hide anything from God. He sees *everything* and you will have to account for your actions."

Okay, got it. Don't have sex. In fact, don't even sort of have sex. Because if you do, scary monster god will make you pregnant and then you will have to show your private parts to all sorts of people and then the entire church will know about your private parts and talk about your private parts, and also your dad will lose his job.

I was only six years old, but I had been duly inducted into whitemalegod's reign of terror.

whitemalegod's tiny terrifying circle of acceptability

Niccolò Machiavelli, the Italian Renaissance politician, famously said, "It is better to be feared than loved." I bet this quote is tattooed on whitemalegod's cold, stony heart, for this is exactly his modus operandi. What better way to control people than to make sure they fear disobeying you?

Whitemalegod's liturgy is fear. In order to control us, he reigns with terror rather than love. As I learned as a child, if anyone violates any of whitemalegod's confusing rules, they will be punished, exposed, shamed, and excommunicated. In order to stay in whitemalegod's good graces, you must perfectly adhere to his rules. One misstep, one outburst, one willful decision and you will be cast out.

Meanwhile, whitemalegod cunningly disguises his reign of terror within a seductive love story.

"For God so loved the world," he claims.

"All are welcome at my table," he invites.

"Come boldly before my throne of grace," he entices.

Whitemalegod manipulates these otherwise beautiful statements in order to lure us into his fold. Once trapped, his actions tell a different story. As the godhead of the white patriarchy hierarchy, he alone occupies the moral high ground. He alone gets to decide what is good and what is evil, who is sacred and who is profane, who belongs and who is cast out, whose efforts will be rewarded and who will languish into learned helplessness. For example, he alone gets to decide how conflict will be addressed—with war and a punitive judicial system. He alone determines what forms of gender and sexual identities are acceptable—cisgender and heterosexual. He gets to decide which interpretations of scripture are orthodox—the interpretations of cis-het white men. He gets to decide which sexual behaviors are pure—monotonous, monogamous, married missionary–style. He gets to decide what constitutes strong leadership—the top-down, executive leadership of cis white men. He gets to decide which entrepreneurs get funded and which university professors earn tenure—the ones whose work supports whitemalegod's white patriarchy. He gets to decide which economic system is most pure—capitalism. By the time we discover that whitemalegod is the patron of conditional acceptance, we are already desperately invested in earning his favor.

Whitemalegod's moral high ground leaves a lot of people out. Indeed, his circle of acceptability is tinier than a pinpoint. He only offers the tantalizing fruits of his table to those who successfully embody the values of white patriarchy—obedience to the social order, staying in one's lane, productivity at all costs, controlling oneself and others, and perfect adherence to whitemalegod's moral codes.

But it's all just a mind game. Because even if one does all of the things that whitemalegod requires, one can still find themselves inhumanly crammed into the hold of a filthy, infested slave ship, as my Black ancestors know. And no matter what hoops you jump through, one might still find themselves locked away in whitemalegod's punitive criminal justice system, as many unjustly incarcerated Black and brown people know. And even if you do everything you can to be an "upstanding" Black woman, you can be unjustly executed by whitemalegod's police force in your own home, as Breonna Taylor knows.

This is because whitemalegod's circle of acceptability is tiny; it is only available to those he has deemed good. The more you embody or approximate his white maleness, the more you are good and potentially granted access to his tiny circle of acceptability. That means Black people are out. Period. The same is true for women, non-binary, and trans folks. No matter how hard we try, no matter how much we silence our divine racial and gender identities, no matter how much we painfully contort ourselves into whitemalegod clones, we will always inevitably fall short of his exacting standard of *perfect white maleness*. We may be able to hang around the edges of the circle for a minute but we all eventually discover that whitemalegod's white boys club remains elusive.

In fact, it remains perfectly elusive—a cycle of terror that keeps all of us striving for love and acceptance that we will never receive. Even the most stellar cis white men can't truly gain access. Not too long ago, I caught one of my most world-renowned, highest-ranking colleagues at Duke in a rare, vulnerable moment in which he admitted that he is driven to (over)produce to the point of exhaustion because he fears he's not good enough.

I responded, "Dude, if you're not good enough, then the rest of us are fucked." But that's how whitemalegod controls us, by convincing all of us—even those, like my colleague, who most resemble whitemalegod—that we're not enough. We must constantly strive for whitemalegod's version of excellence and conquer our imperfections in order to prove to whitemalegod that we are worthy to sit at his table. But since we're all desperately scrambling to get a seat at a table in whitemalegod's exclusive club, we never stop to ask ourselves: *Do I even want a spot in whitemalegod's tiny circle of acceptability?* No, we're too busy scrambling and trampling others as we chase the acceptance we will never receive. Consequently, we are always at war—with the Earth, with each other, and with ourselves—in whitemalegod's police state.

Whitemalegod's tiny circle of acceptability is also terrifying because, as I learned as a child, when one fails to meet whitemalegod's expectations, one is cast out violently and dramatically. Whitemalegod is a petulant dictator who knows his power is illegitimate and is constantly afraid of a coup. He's a narcissist with high-but-unstable self-esteem. Though he holds all the cards in our society, he is perpetually afraid of losing control. That's why he needs us to stay in line and assure him that he truly is the king of the universe. We don't get to embrace our divinity-humanity and make our own choices about what is good, what is true, and what to do with our bodies because independence is a threat to his patriarchal power. So, when he excommunicates us for failing to conform to his rules, he has to make a chilling spectacle that terrifies everyone else back into line.

It's all about the spectacle of terror. It's why spiritual communities publicly shame people who fail to meet their moral standards. It's why families label and then excommunicate people who are deemed "black sheep." It's why corporations squash whistleblowers. It's why the US military–industrial complex exists. And it's why white cops put dozens of bullets in unarmed Black people's bodies. It's all about the spectacle of terror as a way to scare us straight and also to demonstrate that the tiny, terrifying circle of acceptability is not just about acceptance; it's also about security. If we cross the line, we will lose both acceptance and security. Whitemalegod wants us to know that excommunication from his tiny, terrifying circle of acceptability can have disastrous consequences on our livelihoods and even our lives.

The father-pastor at my childhood church was an ardent disciple of whitemalegod. This is evident in his need to control his adult daughter, police her body, and expose her to the church. When he felt that he had lost control of his daughter, he responded with horrific violence. This is perfectly in line with whitemalegod's machiavellian monster practices. A true patriarch is in perfect control of his progeny, and whitemalegod is the patriarch of patriarchs. He must remain in full control or he violently falls apart, lashing out at us as he tumbles.

Black historians such as Kelly Brown Douglas and Howard Thurman teach us that white slave masters used similar tactics to instill fear in and control my enslaved ancestors. The white masters, like whitemalegod, were unjustly and immorally trafficking and exploiting enslaved people. Not surprisingly, my enslaved ancestors resisted by rebelling, attempting to run away, or, more often, slowing down on the job, deliberately breaking tools, and pretending that they couldn't comprehend instructions. In other words, my enslaved ancestors were exercising their divine right to do whatever the fuck they wanted to do. As a way of controlling the enslaved people, slaveholders used machiavellian tactics to terrorize the enslaved people back into submission. These tactics included whipping enslaved people for trifling things like appearing unhappy, creating actual laws called *slave codes* that required enslaved people to respect and obey the slaveholders, and using religion and constant intimidation to shame enslaved people into compliance.[1] Like whitemalegod and the father-pastor, the petulant white slave masters would not tolerate insubordination or affirm that each human has a right to exercise their personal agency. So, they scared them into submission.

enslaved by whitemalegod

The Scarlet Letter experience at my childhood church scared me into submission too. I didn't want to be publicly shamed as that young woman had been, so I devoted myself to doing exactly what whitemalegod's white patriarchy requires: obedience to the social order, staying in my lane, productivity at all costs, controlling myself and others, and perfect adherence to whitemalegod's moral codes. This meant not speaking out on behalf of my humanity and the humanity of others. For example, even though everything I knew about racism I had learned in the Christian church, I remained devoted to it because I was forever afraid that if I made a choice for myself, like the woman had done at my childhood church, I would be excommunicated and no longer able to strive for that elusive acceptance and security that whitemalegod would never truly confer upon me.

For several years, I attended a church that is part of the Vineyard Movement, a "global" group of churches that gentrified the Holy Spirit. In the 1970s, people from various Vineyard churches ripped the Spirit from Her liberating and wild environs among the world's most marginalized people, sanitized Her, and began serving Her venti-skim-pumpkin-spice-latte style to white suburbanites. The particular Vineyard church I attended in the Minneapolis metro area called itself a "multiethnic church" and proudly named racial justice as one of its core values. But in actuality, it was whiter than a Minnesota winter and more likely to exploit than nurture its few Black attendees. Tokenism was a pillar of its culture of exploitation. In an apparent effort to *appear* more diverse, the predominantly white leadership put pressure on me and other Black members to serve in powerless but public capacities—deliver the church announcements during Sunday service, play violin in the music ensemble, sing a Gospel solo, and so on. Yet when Black members pointed out actual structural racism within the church, our concerns were met with platitudes and inaction. Despite my increasing awareness of this reality, I not only attended but actually volunteered as an unpaid leader and preacher because I felt compelled to prove my worth in a world that would never value me. It was my very own *Little Plantation on the Prairie*.

Though whitemalegod's tiny, terrifying circle of acceptability torments us, we remain on the plantation because it's all we know, and we are afraid of what will happen if we try to escape. I didn't know who I would be without the church community and I definitely didn't know what my moral standing would be if I chose another path. So, like the dutiful Mammy that I was, I remained on the plantation, striving and serving my little Black heart out.

I could have stayed on the plantation forever, but the Sacred Black Feminine beckoned me through the voice of Chanequa Walker-Barnes. In her book *Too Heavy a Yoke: Black Women and the Burden of Strength*, Walker-Barnes showed me that my specific attempts to gain access to whitemalegod's tiny, terrifying circle of acceptability was one of the ways that whitemalegod maintains control of Black women.

Before I finished the first paragraph of the introduction, I had already melted into sobs because I knew this book was about me. In *Too Heavy a Yoke*, Walker-Barnes, a psychologist and theologian, explains that society insists "that to be a good Black woman—a *StrongBlackWoman*—is to be stoic in the face of struggle, to devote oneself to taking care of others' needs at the expense of one's own, and to show no signs of needing support of any kind from others." Pop culture examples of the StrongBlackWoman are Dr. Miranda Bailey on *Grey's Anatomy* or Tyler Perry's Madea whom Walker-Barnes calls "the StrongBlackWoman on steroids." In her description of the StrongBlackWoman, Walker-Barnes gave me the language to consciously name how whitemalegod's toxic trifecta of racism, sexism, and classism landed on my Black female body and kept me on his plantation.

In her book, Walker-Barnes expertly shows that the StrongBlackWoman identity was initially introduced by leaders of the Black racial uplift movement at the turn of the twentieth century as a way to combat the insidious stereotypes that have plagued Black women since we were forcibly brought to America: the asexual and happily oppressed *Mammy*, the sexually promiscuous and manipulative *Jezebel*, and the sharp-tongued and emasculating *Sapphire*.

Walker-Barnes writes, "This required the suppression and denial of any weakness, shortcomings, or vulnerabilities that might confirm or underscore racial stereotypes."[2]

Ultimately, this goal wasn't achieved; the Mammy, Jezebel, and Sapphire stereotypes remain alive and well in whitemalegod's world today. Meanwhile, the StrongBlackWoman identity, which at first glance seems like a positive identity, has wreaked havoc on Black women's emotional, physical, spiritual, and relational health. By contorting ourselves into the StrongBlackWoman identity, we silence our divine Black female humanity with its glorious strengths and vulnerabilities. Not surprisingly, silencing our humanity hurts us. Throughout the book, Walker-Barnes presents overwhelming research showing that the StrongBlackWoman identity is associated with exhaustion, obesity, addiction, anxiety, and nonreciprocal relationships.

For the last century, Black women have embraced the hard-working, stoic, sacrificial ethic of the StrongBlackWoman and covered up any signs of weakness or vulnerability in order to show the world that Black women *aren't* immoral, lazy, and selfish, and to hopefully finally gain entrance to whitemalegod's tiny, terrifying circle of acceptability. But ultimately, we've all been played because we are still perceived as wholly unholy and we remain outside the circle. In an attempt to escape one set of racist/sexist/classist stereotypes, Black women have run smack dab into another stereotype, one that is maintained by the same cocktail of racism, sexism, and classism.

As I read Walker-Barnes's liberating words, I realized that the StrongBlackWoman is simply a modern-day Mammy. I also realized that I had been striving to be the StrongBlack-Woman for years, while I was getting played by whitemale-god and his minions, and that no matter how much I labored to prove my acceptability, worth, and purity, they would never fully embrace me. I would always remain outside of whitemalegod's tiny, terrifying circle of acceptability.

So, I took my first major step toward freedom and quit the Little Plantation on the Prairie church. I had no idea where I was going; my entire social and spiritual worlds were wrapped up in my whitemalegod church life. But as Sue Monk Kidd teaches us, patriarchal religion controls us by convincing us that the Earth is flat—that if we sail off toward the unknown spiritual horizon, we will fall off the Earth. But the truth is that the Earth is round. When we sail toward the

unknown, we don't fall off. Instead, we come full circle—
stronger, wiser, and more connected to unconditional Love
than ever.[3]

severing my career as christianity's house nigger

I sure hoped to encounter Love's full circle because I needed
Love more than ever. I soon realized that the Little Plantation
on the Prairie church was simply the first of many Christian
plantations I needed to escape. And I quickly learned that
with each subsequent escape, the stakes heightened.

As I left the Little Plantation on the Prairie and began to
explore the Sacred Black Feminine, it quickly became clear
that my livelihood, which was solely sourced by whitemalegod's institutions, was in jeopardy. As a faculty member at
Duke Divinity School, I knew that my "witchy" exploration into the Sacred Black Feminine would ruffle feathers
and threaten my job. As a monthly columnist for *Christianity
Yesterday* magazine, I knew that my lucrative speaking and
freelance writing career would wither away if evangelicals
discovered that I had ventured away from spiritual suburbia
and into the forbidden thicket of the Sacred Black Feminine. I
knew that my exploration into the unknown would make me
an untouchable in the mainstream Christian community—
the community that had reliably paid my bills.

In early 2017, I was presented with a chance to make
another escape when the white president of an enormous
Christian seminary called me and asked for my help. You
see, he had a bit of a mess on his hands. It had been highly

publicized that the vast majority of white Christians had voted for racist, misogynist Trump, and now the world's worst kept secret—that the majority of white Christians are racist and misogynist—was out. When you're the head of an institution that trains a significant number of white Christian leaders, this presents a bit of a PR nightmare. In response to his distress, the president's solution was to write a book that distanced him and his institution from "those racists" by explaining why the "true" tenets of Christianity are exactly the opposite of Trump's political platform. He was calling because he wanted me and a handful of others to co-author the book with him. He needed help cleaning up his mess.

"Will you join me in fighting back and setting the record straight?" he probed.

Though I am not a white Christian, and this wasn't my mess to clean up, I wasn't surprised by his request. I'd spent the past ten years cultivating a large public platform in the Christian world. And as a Black woman, I didn't achieve that kind of success without cleaning up a lot of white people's messes.

For example, a group at Lifeway Christian Resources, a ginormous, Nashville-based Christian media company, invited me to appear on one of their television programs. When I landed at the Nashville airport, the producer texted me to say that no one was available to pick me up from the airport and that I should take a taxi. Not exactly southern hospitality, but I didn't think anything of it. When I arrived at the Lifeway studio, I saw a handful of white men standing around doing nothing. Not one to hold back on cutting humor, I quipped, "It looks like there were plenty of people available to pick me up from the airport." After a long, uncomfortable silence, one of the men said, "Well, all of the women who work here are at a women's chapel right now and it's against company policy for male employees to ride alone in cars with women."

"Oh," I said, "Well, it's a good thing you have that policy because I definitely made out with the cab driver on my way over here."

But my sarcasm simply masked my hurt. Though I tried to share my perspective with the men in that studio, my words ricocheted off their hard hearts. They couldn't hear that such a policy is oppressive to women because it assumes women are the problem—that, as a woman, I was a predator who might "cause" a man to do something immoral if I just get him alone. I told them they needed to reevaluate and reform their gender-based practices. And then, regrettably, I stayed for the interview. I should have walked out on their misogynistic asses, but I stayed so as not to make a scene.

Cleaning up white people's messes.

When Campus Crusade for Christ, a global nonprofit with an overwhelmingly white executive leadership team and a history of racial tensions,[4] was deservedly accused of systemic racism, the organization flew me down to their plantationlike headquarters to lead a retreat for its racist board of directors. While facilitating the retreat, it was clear to me that the almost exclusively white board was woefully ignorant of the racial oppression that the BIPOC (Black, Indigenous, and People of Color) staff experienced within the organization. Even worse, as I began to share the harrowing stories I had received firsthand from BIPOC staff, many of the board members became defensive, suggesting that these disgruntled staff needed an attitude adjustment. As someone who has worked with numerous boards on racial equity, I believed that this board was not in a position to lead meaningful change. Nevertheless, news of my time with the board spread throughout the organization, giving a false impression that the board was actively working toward racial equity. "See, we're working on it," the public optics suggested. But then the organization proceeded to *not* work on it. Though I was privy to this blatant hypocrisy, I kept my mouth shut because the organization paid well, and I wanted to keep getting work.

Cleaning up white people's messes.

In the months leading up to Urbana, a massive "missions" conference for which I was a token Black speaker, I increasingly recognized that the organization hosting the conference was homophobic, anti-Black, money driven, and imperialistic. Nevertheless, I proceeded to speak on "unity" to the seventeen thousand attendees, convincing myself that, despite these blatant issues, my voice could make a difference. My keynote address was well received, and I was heralded as a true voice for justice. Months later, it was reported that the organization fired employees who would not affirm its homophobic theology. Justice my ass.

Cleaning up white people's messes.

I repeatedly acquiesced when the heavy-handed editors at *Christianity Today* magazine blunted every single one of my sharp-shooting monthly columns to the point that I no longer recognized my own writing. This way, they could proudly claim to have a Black columnist without actually subjecting their white readership to actual Black thought. I saw the sinister reason why I was chosen to be a monthly columnist, but the gig opened up speaking and consulting opportunities.

Cleaning up white people's messes. It's how I attempted access to whitemalegod's tiny, terrifying circle of acceptability in order to access power and make a living.

And it was a good living. On the surface, there's quite a bit of money and power in being a modern-day house nigger. I was speaking on some of the biggest stages, offered a seat at some of the most exclusive boardroom tables, and earning a six-figure income.

But the thing about being a house nigger is that you're still enslaved.

Oh, it may seem like laboring in the "big house" is better than picking tobacco out in the sun-drenched field, but at the end of the day, neither house nigger nor field nigger is free. Deep inside I instinctively understood that Christianity would only continue to pretend to give me power as long as I stayed in my lane and toed the party line. I knew that the only reason I was able to maintain my "success" in that world was because I often did not speak up on behalf of my humanity and pain—because I often did not walk away from opportunities to clean up white people's messes.

Regardless of how attractive they may have appeared to outside observers or what narrative I told myself at the time, the "opportunities" I was given were not invitations to boldly speak my Sacred Black Feminine truth to power. They were opportunities to contribute to the project of making Christianity look good despite its woeful, interminable, and well-deserved reputation for being imperialistic, anti-Black, and misogynistic. In other words, Christianity doesn't have a PR problem; it has a whitemalegod problem.

As I recalled the countless messes I had cleaned up on Christianity's behalf, I felt a wave of grief. I had succumbed to the plantation religion of the whitemalegod who is printed on the money, embraced my house nigger identity, and, in doing so, had betrayed myself.

I was getting played.

So, in response to the seminary president's invitation to clean up white people's messes yet again by contributing to his book, I put on my awesome Bose noise-cancelling head-phones (paid for by that house nigga money), pressed play on my "Boi Bye Christianity" Spotify playlist, and sang along to Big Sean's "I Don't Fuck with You" while I sent the seminary president an email saying *No* with a capital N.

I got a million trillion things I'd rather fuckin' do
Than to be fuckin' with you.

9

She Who Loves by Letting Go

guess Big Sean is a prophet because it turns out I really did have a million trillion things I'd rather fuckin' do. Saying no to cleaning up Christianity's messes opened up space for spiritual riches that I couldn't have imagined much less experienced if I had continued fuckin' with Christianity's messes.

Make no mistake, escaping the Christian house nigger plantation was a risk that opened up a world of fear and uncertainty. For example, I wasn't sure how I was going to sustain my speaking and writing business now that the invitations were starting to dry up. And within weeks of publicly musing about the problem of an exclusively white-and-male god, much of my modestly sized social media following withered away.

But, as I continued toward liberation, I realized that money and platform were the least of my worries. As I journeyed on, I began to awaken to the truth that the "single plantation escape" is a myth. We never escape one plantation. To escape one plantation is to commit to escaping a thousand subsequent plantations. For once we move beyond what is currently enslaving us, we begin to see the other enslavements. And with each enslavement we are presented with the opportunity to make another difficult choice. Do I keep moving? Or do I fall back?

Escaping the Christian House Nigger plantation was just the beginning. I knew that the toughest escapes from whitemalegod's relational plantations still lay ahead.

Can't Stop, Won't Stop . . . Even for Family

Back in early 2017, when I banned toxic masculinity from my life, I stopped reading books authored by whitemalegod's minions, such as the Apostle Paul, so I'm as shocked as anyone to quote John Bunyan here. But every once in a while, a dead white guy says something that heals.

In *Pilgrim's Progress*, a seventeenth-century allegory, Bunyan tells the story of a man named Christian who decides to embark on an epic pilgrimage in pursuit of true, liberating life. At the start of the book, we find Christian so overtaken by his urgency to begin his journey that he is literally running out of his house and away from all he knows. Bunyan narrates: ". . . the man began to run. He hadn't run far from his own door when his wife and children noticed what he was doing and cried out to him. 'Come back! Come home!' The man put his fingers in his ears and ran on. 'Life! Life! Eternal life!'"[1]

Christian's story has been stirring in me since I read it as a
child. Even then, I related to Christian and wondered if I too
would need to run away from my family. A "good girl" in
a violently patriarchal family, at the time I didn't consciously
understand how abusive my family really was. But I could
sense my constant terror and loneliness and I longed to break
free. Decades later, as I settled into my pilgrimage life in the
Auvergne, I simmered with the urgency Christian exuded as
he plugged his ears, ran away from all of the loved ones who
tried to hold him back, and screamed "Life! Life! Eternal life!"
I was struck by the fact that his family and close friends were
actually holding him back on his journey toward true life.
After all, family members and other beloveds are supposed to
be cheering us on as we seek healing and liberation.

But this wasn't the case for Christian. In fact, his first obstacles to liberation were not a lack of money, physical injury,
or even hostile strangers and animals. Though he would encounter those impediments on his long and harrowing journey toward freedom, his first obstacles were the loved ones
who tried to prevent him from even beginning his journey.

I felt a kinship with Christian; the primary obstacles to
my ongoing liberation were not money, social media platform, or even the loss of the broader spiritual communities
to which I belonged. Heartbreakingly, the primary obstacles
were the people closest to me. They were the only temp-
tation that could compel me to return. Though losing my
lucrative speaking income stung, I still had my Duke job
and a roof over my head. And, honestly, the loss of thousands of social media followers felt more like a cleansing than

anything else. I had long grown wary of my white Christian followers and their anemic performative allyship.

No, if I was going to turn back at this point, it would be in order to save my cherished relationships with my family and lifelong friends. Like Christian, most of my family and friends were unable to support me on my journey, much less accompany me. And I quickly realized that most of my close relationships were governed by whitemalegod's slickest brand of white patriarchy—the kind that convinces you that faithfulness means silencing the urge to run toward freedom. Faithfulness means staying put. Faithfulness means loyalty to everyone but yourself.

I knew that my liberating journey toward the Sacred Black Feminine would require more than simply saying no to speaking invitations. It would require that I completely release or rewire my beloved relationships. No more hierarchy, no more toxic enmeshment, no more relationships that required me to hide *any* of my gloriously divine Black female self.

Like Christian, I felt the urge to plug my ears and run away from my beloveds screaming, "Life! Life! Eternal life!" But first I needed to recognize and escape the machiavellian's monster fear-control cycle in my relational life.

Fear and Control: Two Sides of the Same Coin

Growing up, spiritual leadership was all about authority and control. For people striving for membership in whitemalegod's tiny, terrifying circle of acceptability, "leadership" often involves policing people's beliefs and actions. Since everyone is petrified of being shamed and excommunicated for failing to adhere to whitemalegod's impossible standards, they devote all their energy to controlling themselves and the people they care about. Further, as whitemalegod is the machiavellian monster whose own fear triggers in him a desire to maniacally control us, we are conditioned to follow in his footsteps. Consequently, when we experience fear, we try to maniacally control ourselves and others. To be spiritual in whitemalegod's world involves contorting yourself into whatever whitemalegod wants you to be and hoping you can successfully jump through his ridiculous hoops. So, to be a spiritual *leader* in whitemalegod's world involves forcing other people to contort themselves too.

Since whitemalegod is the fatherskygod "out there somewhere," he is distant from us and uses "priests" to mediate his relationship with us. Consequently, women need husbands to control them, congregants need pastors to discipline them, and kids need parents to police their bodies. The concept of consent is completely absent in this hierarchal structure. If you want to avoid being shamed and excommunicated, you do whatever whitemalegod's minion is telling you to do without ever asking yourself: *Do I want to do this?*

This system of "priestly policing" is exemplified in the evangelical purity movement. Born into a conservative Black Christian family in 1980, I experienced the brunt of purity culture, one of whitemalegod's most cunning doctrines of fear and control. When I was fifteen, I kissed my first boy, a true sweetie named David. Within hours of learning of my kiss, my parents, stricken with fear, somberly presented me with a purity ring. The ring was technically a gift, but it felt like a threat because it was accompanied with an admonition to "save myself for marriage." Rather than celebrating the beautiful milestone experience of a first kiss and inviting me into a discussion about how I wanted to relate to my body in this new phase of physical intimacy, they sought to control me. And lucky for them, they had lots of help.

Between the Southern Baptist denomination's "True Love Waits" propaganda machine and a terrorist manifesto written by a young conservative Christian called *I Kissed Dating Goodbye*, I had duly learned that if I engaged in any sexual intimacy before marriage, I would be damaged goods—unwanted and irredeemable. I had already seen what they did to the young pregnant unmarried woman at my childhood church. I knew what my fate would be if I violated the rules. But the rules were blurry. In whitemalegod's anti-body culture, we never talked about what actually constitutes sex. I guessed that simple kisses were sort of okay, though they definitely triggered an alarm for my parents. But what about making out, heavy petting, mutual masturbation, and oral sex? I was confused. I wanted to be "pure," but I didn't exactly know what that looked like. Consequently, I never knew if I had "crossed a line" in my romantic relationships and was plagued with fear and shame until years later when I broke free.

Though I was confused about what constitutes pure versus impure behavior, I was not confused about how much fear and shame I should carry if I didn't meet my parents' and whitemalegod's purity standards. You see, this is how whitemalegod continues to rule us—by teaching us that the moral authority exists outside ourselves. We don't get to determine what is pure or impure, whitemalegod and his priests do. Thoroughly conditioned by whitemalegod, my parents continued to exercise spiritual authority over me well into my thirties. When they feared for my safety or purity, they shamed and fearmongered me back into the fold.

In my twenties, when a loving, consensual relationship with an older man ended, my mom told me that, throughout the length of my relationship, she had repeatedly experienced a burning sensation in her vaginal area. Mom explained that she believed the burning sensation was a sign from God that I had crossed a line in my adult relationship. Eagerly embodying whitemalegod's priest model, Mom used the fact that God "spoke" to her as a reason to interrogate me about my sexual interactions with the man. When I reluctantly confessed to engaging in oral sex, she told me she was "heartbroken but that she forgave me." She added that she believed I could still be pure if I returned to my previous commitment to "saving myself for marriage." Interactions like this confirmed that, even as an adult, Mom and Dad were the spiritual leaders to whom I was accountable. They also communicated that I was not the moral authority when it came to my body—they were. Only Mom and Dad had the power to forgive me and determine if I was still redeemable. They were whitemalegod's priests and I believed I was required to submit to them.

At the time, I didn't recognize this type of interference as a form of abuse. But psychologist Tina Schermer Sellers has studied purity culture and discovered that "the self-loathing that [women exposed to purity culture] were feeling and describing about themselves really paralleled the kind of self-loathing that you often see with somebody who's experienced childhood sexual assault."[2]

It was self-loathing that kept me chained to this abusive priest model of morality. After engaging in sexual activity, I'd be so wracked with shame that I would circle back to the "rules" and try to contort myself into something that would be acceptable to whitemalegod and his priests. Though I didn't have penal-vaginal sex until I was thirty-four years old, I always feared that what I had been told was true: that I was damaged goods, unwanted and irredeemable. I constantly feared that I would be publicly shamed and cast out like the young unmarried pregnant woman at my childhood church.

And I never once asked myself: What do I want? What is good and pure to me? What information do I want to share with my parents and what do I want to keep to myself? Whitemalegod's liturgy of fear and control completely ruled me. The self-loathing kept me caged in whitemalegod's abusive torment and also prevented me from connecting with my inner moral compass. In fact, I convinced myself that since I was so shameful, I couldn't trust my desires. My only way to holiness was to follow whitemalegod's commands.

Trapped in self-loathing, the only thing I knew to do was mimic the fear-control pattern that had been modeled for me. When I feared for the safety and purity of others, I used shame and fearmongering to police their behaviors. As a college student under the spell of whitemalegod, I believed that to be a spiritual leader meant to constantly point out my peers' waywardness, "hold people accountable," and generally lord over them. I remember summoning a group of friends to my dorm room late one night in order to drop self-righteous shame bombs on them. It was my opinion that they were drinking too much, dating the wrong people, and not taking their morality seriously enough. I was afraid they were going down the wrong path. Like my parents, I allowed my fear to energize my need to control these friends. Apparently, it was my place to chastise them and assault them with my moral standards. I was whitemalegod in blackface.

"Life! Life! Eternal Life!"

As I journeyed toward the Sacred Black Feminine, I awakened to the way that rampant white patriarchy governed my relationship with my parents. I knew I needed to relinquish my deeply entrenched identity as the perfect daughter who always strived to obey quickly and quietly, as I was taught. I longed to get out from under the boot of their moral authority and establish my own spiritual path, one that significantly diverged from theirs. As I began taking steps away, I discovered with horror that, much like Christian in *Pilgrim's Progress*, my initial steps were jarring and clunky. Breaking away from a long-standing abusive relational pattern is never tidy. I struggled to speak my truth and my parents struggled to understand why my truth now differed from theirs. But over time, and with the help of therapy and a deeper connection to the Sacred Black Feminine within me, I learned to communicate new boundaries by politely but firmly saying things like, "Mom and Dad, I'm not going to discuss that topic with you" or "I don't feel safe in that spiritual community, so I'm not going to attend that event with you." Every time I spoke my truth and set a boundary, I felt like I was awkwardly running out the door, screaming "Life! Life! Eternal Life!" while my loving but bewildered parents labored to understand why my life path required that I run away.

Indeed, my journey toward freedom did require a downshift in our felt intimacy. When we were patriarchally intertwined, our relationship seemed intimate because I consistently submitted to their authority and confined myself to their spiritual world. My whole adult life, I indiscriminately shared everything with them—my hopes, fears, heartbreak, mistakes, and decision-making processes—and submitted to their moral authority. Once I broke free, I found we had very little in common. No longer looking to them for spiritual mentorship nor willing to share details about my intimate experiences, questions, and challenges, our hierarchical relationship fell apart and was replaced with pleasant but impersonal conversation. Further, we no longer spoke the same spiritual language, so we struggled to communicate from the heart. The new way seemed healthier and safer to me, but I grieved the loss of felt intimacy.

I know my beloved dad grieved it too. A few months before my walking pilgrimage, I shared with him a few of the things I had been learning about the divine feminine. Though he listened graciously and earnestly, his face telegraphed his fear. I could plainly see that he was afraid to lose me. He was afraid that while forging my own path to the Divine, I would get lost without his guidance and protection. In that moment, I imagined him in the suburban neighborhood of my dream. Dad was wildly and desperately reaching for me, like he wanted to come with me on my journey into the woods. But he couldn't follow me because he was chained to a towering whitemalegod monument in the center of the neighborhood. As I squinted, I could make out the inscription on the monument: "I'm the father! You will not go into those woods without me! I'm the father!" He was trapped in his own patriarchy, unable to enjoy the intimacy and camaraderie with me for which he so longed.

Glancing at his chains, I resisted the urge to run back to him, to soothe his fear and assure him I would *never* venture into the woods without him. I knew that my next step toward liberation required that I relinquish my deeply ingrained desire to keep Dad happy at the expense of my spiritual well-being. Before I said another word to my dad, I closed my eyes and envisioned Our Lady of the Good Death, the Black Madonna of Clermont-Ferrand, who I only knew from books at that point. Her glorious image and title reminded me that death leads to life, that I can trust that anything that dies on the liberation path will lead to regenerative life.

With deep sorrow, I said to Dad, "I know I'm moving in a direction that scares you. However, I've spent my whole life trying to anticipate, meet, and even exceed your needs and expectations. I'm not going back into that prison."

Dad slumped in his chair, stunned.

Later that day when I returned to my home, I thought

of ol' Christian from *Pilgrim's Progress* and repeated aloud to myself, "Life! Life! Eternal Life!" As I said the words again and again, an embodied longing for both Life *and* real intimacy with my cherished parents burst to the surface, birthing a waterfall from my eyes. As I allowed the emotion to move through my being, my tears turned to heaving, full-body sobs. Feeling immensely alone and afraid, I staggered over to my living room wall, where a tattered, early nineteenth-century oil painting of the Black Madonna hung. Reaching for intimacy with Her, I placed both hands on the painting. As I caressed Her cracked and peeling body, I knew I could trust Her to hold my longing with care and also to lead me forward.

Lead me, She did. Just months later, I discovered that my decision to re-wire my relationship with my dad led me right into the arms of the Virgin-Warrior, the God of Consent who loves by letting go.

The Virgin-Warrior

Though I had begun speaking my truth, changing the DNA of a lifelong, enmeshed father-daughter relationship is easier said than done. For one, it involves a lot of grief and loss. I grieved when my dad and I became more and more distant as I asserted myself more. I grieved when my dad seemed lost when I asked him to stop acting as my spiritual authority and, instead, embrace mutual, adult friendship with me. I grieved when I realized it was not safe to share everything with Dad and Mom as I had dutifully done my entire life. I grieved when I experienced momentous life events and could not

share them with my parents because to do so would expose me to their spiritual abuse. And I felt the loss of having
parents so beholden to whitemalegod's liturgy of fear that
they could not unconditionally and nonjudgmentally hold
space for my varied life experiences. I knew that a patriarchal
allegiance to my parents would make it impossible for me to
do the upcoming liberation work of fearlessly examining the
way whitemalegod ruled my childhood home. And I grieved
that I had to choose liberation over felt intimacy with my
cherished parents.

I was still carrying all this grief and loss months later when
I walked eighteen miles to the tiny village of Thuret to visit
the Black Madonna who is famously known as the Virgin-
Warrior. When I first fantasized about a long walking pilgrimage across central France, I imagined expansive blue skies,
poetic country roads, and rolling green hills as far as the eye
could see. Well, some days were like that, for the Auvergne region is extraordinarily beautiful and rural. But the day I walked
to the Virgin-Warrior was the opposite of idyllic. Indeed, the
stormy journey matched the storm of grief in my heart.

I left my apartment before dawn and spent the morning
walking through miles of ghastly urban sprawl. By lunch-
time, I had reached the countryside that lay just outside
Clermont-Ferrand. However, rather than encountering
adorable medieval French villages with cobblestone streets
and eight-hundred-year-old buildings, my walking route
took me smack dab through the heart of an industrial farm-
ing community. Agricultural drones buzzed noisily above as
I lumbered by massive, evil-looking barns that practically

screamed "We are full of GMOs! We're killing the planet!"
To make matters worse, there were no poetic roads! None.
As I walked miles and miles along a major thoroughfare, the
wind picked up and the winter rain began to fall. Nevertheless, I trudged along, my bright red coat getting baptized in
the muddy, oily muck that the tractor-trailer trucks kicked
up as they whizzed by me.

In the late afternoon, just I was nearing Thuret, the gusts
of wind became violently strong and my pace slowed. My
face stung as the wind repeatedly slapped it and I had to
lower my left shoulder like an offensive lineman attempting
a block in order to just keep moving forward. I was exhausted and wet and hangry, but I was determined to see
this Virgin-Warrior I had read about. She was the Black
Madonna who defied everything I had learned about purity
and authority.

I was especially excited to meet Her because my research
had begun to uncover many of the ways that whitemalegod
has weaponized Mary's virginity. Not surprisingly, the purity
culture in which I was raised is rooted in patriarchy's policing of Mary. According to tradition, Mary was impregnated
by the Holy Spirit and bore the Christ Child; no man was
involved. This reality threatened patriarchy, which petulantly
needs men to be the heroes of every story. Patriarchy couldn't
handle a woman singlehandedly bearing the Divine. So, patriarchy reduced Mary to her virginity, ignoring her fiery, divine,
truth-telling in the Magnificat (Luke 1) and recasting her as a
weak (white) woman whose participation in the story of God
was contingent upon her "purity." Consequently, virginity

became the standard of purity for all women and a way for patriarchy to terrorize and control women.

As I learned more about the Virgin-Warrior of Thuret, I uncovered more hidden truth. For centuries, saints who were devoted to Mary, such as St. Bernard of Clairvaux, believed Mary to be a human form of God. In fact, many understood her virginity to have little to do with her sexual activity and everything to do with the fact that no male seed was involved in the birthing of God. These saints and other Mary devotees call her the Life Spring, the Source of All Power and Grace, the Source-without-Source, and the human form of the Creator.[3] According to them, she birthed God as a virgin because she *is* God.[4]

As I walked the final stormy mile to Thuret, I pondered the Virgin-Warrior's liberating origin story. She was called a Virgin because she was the Source of All Life. And it was precisely Her "virginity" that also made her a Warrior. She was immeasurably powerful because no men, priests, parents, or other assorted whitemalegod minions could add to, subtract from, or otherwise control Her divine power. The Virgin-Warrior was 100 percent free of whitemalegod's tiny, terrifying circle of acceptability. She was Her own woman, divine in Her own right.

As I finally entered the six-hundred-inhabitant village, I imagined the thousands of pilgrims who, since the 1200s, have walked across mountain ranges, through dangerously stormy weather, and during extraordinarily violent eras in order to visit the Virgin-Warrior. Like me, many of these pilgrims experienced whitemalegod's systemic oppression and visited the Virgin-Warrior in hopes of healing, empowerment, and liberation. Unlike me, these pilgrims didn't have Patagonia jackets, waterproof Keen hiking boots, and high-performance winter gloves to help them survive the journey. They didn't have Uber as a backup option in case they got tired or injured on the way. Like Christian in *Pilgrim's Progress*, their dangerous journey toward Her was powered by a desperate grasping for "Life! Life! Eternal Life!" As I approached the old church where the Virgin-Warrior lived, I paid homage to these nameless pilgrims. As a fellow seeker of Life, I knew I was in good company.

She Who Rises from the Mud

As soon as I entered the empty village church, I plopped down on a rock-hard antique pew. Exhausted, I rested my cramping thighs before I began making my way around the stony, gray interior in search of Her. Much to my surprise, I didn't have to look hard. Unlike many Black Madonnas, who are tucked in some dark, out-of-the-way corner of a church, the Virgin-Warrior was prominently seated at the front of the church. She was magnificent. A gold crown on Her head, Her extra-dark-chocolate face boasted a defiant stare that taunted, "Go ahead, I dare you to tell me about myself." Even Her Christ Child who, rather than being an infant, looked to be about preschool aged and mimicked Her defiance. It was clear the Virgin-Warrior and Her mean-mugging Toddler Jesus weren't having any of whitemalegod's controlling tactics. But as I stood before Her, I noticed something I hadn't noticed in the pictures of Her I had seen. At the base of Her statue, stood four giant lotus flowers.

"Hmmm, lotus flowers." I murmured to myself.

In my meditation practice, I had encountered Thich Nhat Hanh's "No mud, no lotus" teaching in which the Vietnamese activist, teacher, and monk shared that the lotus flower only grows in the mud. The lotus flower rises from all that is considered dirty, impure, and unacceptable.

I smiled as I looked up at Her ornate lotus flowers and then down at my once-red jacket now covered in roadside mud. I had walked through mud to get to Her—both the relational mud of choosing a different path than my parents as well as the physical mud of walking eighteen miles in search of the One who would help me connect with the moral lifespring within me.

As I stood before Her statue, I realized that if the lotus flowers that surrounded Her rose from the mud, then She too rose from the mud. Her defiant stance in the middle of a pit of mud declared an entirely new truth to me about what it means to be pure. Whitemalegod terrorizes us by maintaining full control of what it means to be "pure" and convincing us that if we engage in acts he has deemed unacceptable we will be excommunicated. But by standing firmly in the mud Herself, the Source-without-Source offers a new way.

What whitemalegod calls impure, the Virgin-Warrior proclaims pure. Where whitemalegod slings mud, She showers unconditional love. Where whitemalegod sees mud, She sees a lotus flower rising because just as Her virginity has nothing to do with Her sexual activity, our purity is not about where we are located or what we've done. To Her, purity is about being connected to Her Life Source, which is completely unmarred by white patriarchy's rules, shame, fear, and terror. And since Her Life Source is ever present and ever available, we are always pure. It doesn't matter if we're slogging through what whitemalegod calls *mud*. She's right there with us in the mud proclaiming we are free of white patriarchal control when we embrace our intrinsic purity. She's right there with us in the mud helping us blossom.

Our Lady of the Mud

By reclaiming the mud, the Virgin-Warrior declares that we are free of whitemalegod's reign of terror. No longer can he tell us what is or is not pure. No longer do he and his minions hold the moral high ground. And no longer do we need to remain trapped in his fear-control cycle. And as a Divine Black Woman who has languished under white patriarchy's horrifying purity codes, the Virgin-Warrior has zero interest in controlling us. She knows how the virgin-whore dichotomy has especially hurled mud onto Black women. She knows how quickly unmarried Black mothers and Black LGBTQ+ people are violently threatened. No, this is not Her way. In Her defiant muddy lotus garden, there are no creeds to recite, no community life agreements to sign, no hoops to jump through, and no fear-control cycles whipping us into shape. She simply offers us Her Life Spring so that we may find our own inner life springs. She knows that, as Her beloved children, we too will rise from the mud.

By reclaiming the mud, She also shows us that She understands that life is complex and full of gray areas. Unlike whitemalegod, She's not interested in our blind devotion or our tidy faith. By rising from the divine mud, She's telling us that our belief is too simple if it is simply adherence to a set of rules. She's telling us that the truth that sets us free is beyond the tidy theological beliefs that make us feel safe. She's telling us to bring Her our moral dilemmas. She's telling us to dwell and blossom in the mud with Her.

Black feminist hip-hop scholar Joan Morgan brilliantly uses the style and language of hip-hop to critique white feminism, saying we need "a feminism brave enough to fuck with the grays." Morgan doesn't use this language to shock for shock's sake. Rather, she uses it to draw our attention to the ugly, messy space of life—those times when we are languishing in what feels like a moral milieu. As a Black feminist, Morgan is only interested in a feminism that can accommodate the gray area, that doesn't need to resolve everything right away, that can be relevant to the untidy questions.

By standing in the mud beside us, the Virgin-Warrior is teaching us that moral perfection is not the goal, moral connection is the goal. She's showing us that our pain, our vulnerabilities, and our so-called mistakes don't offend or deter her. Rather, She's inviting us to follow in Her footsteps and connect with Her, our divine life source, no matter where we are. She is our Lady of the Mud, the One whose purity has been attacked for centuries. She entirely exists in the gray, and yet She rises. No, our gray, muddy lives don't scare her. Unlike weak, petulant, easily threatened whitemalegod, the

Virgin-Warrior is the God Who Is Brave Enough to Fuck with the Grays.

More than anything, She loves by letting go. Compared to whitemalegod's reign of terror, Her love is so freeing that Black transgender spiritual teacher Marty S. calls Her/Them the God of Consent. Marty S. writes, "They see us. They know our pain and hear our cries. And They support us as we make the choices that we need to feel safe. That includes both turning away from and turning to Them."[5] She knows that Her Life Spring flows through us too. And She trusts that it will guide us to all that is good.

As I've drawn near the Sacred Black Feminine, I've discovered that She definitely has no need for priests. The matriarchal way is radically different than the patriarchal way because it emphasizes God's immanence, God's accessibility to every single soul. So, the priest/guru model is unnecessary; each person is a priest and can directly connect with God. There is no room for hierarchy or self-righteousness. In the matriarchal way, we don't sling mud at people. We don't shame them into changing.

My encounter with the Virgin-Warrior helped me see that if I truly believe in Her immanent connection to every single soul, then I am also invited to believe that She is capable of connecting with Her children without my help. Rather than self-righteously and fearfully interfering in people's lives as I have done in the past, I can relax into the truth that She is brave enough to fuck with the grays and navigate any spiritual muck in order to reach people. This truth offered me a new model of spiritual leadership that involves loving invitation rather than shaming coercion. As I continued on

my journey and uncovered more of the perils of white patriarchy, my anger and fear boiled, leading me to want to
resort to the controlling ways of whitemalegod by shaming
my loved ones onto my path. But to practice (not just believe in) the Sacred Black Feminine means that I don't get
to police people. Not even the people who have policed me.

As I continued to forge a delicate, new dance with my
parents, I cherished the fact that I could release all my grief
and uncertainty to a God who is brave enough to fuck with
the grays. My steps toward deeper liberation continued to be
clumsy, but since She is brave enough to fuck with the grays,
I knew that She met me and offered me life even in the midst
of the clumsiness. As I relaxed into Her gray, I stopped un-
fairly expecting myself to perfectly finesse each step toward
freedom with my parents. Even more so, as I gave myself
permission to clumsily create a new dance with my parents,
I was better able to honor their humanity by giving them
space to respond with similar clumsiness. They were on their
own journey, and they needed the freedom to learn their
dance steps at their own pace without me pushing them or
colonizing the moral high ground. Though I continued to
set boundaries and make choices that honored my dignity,
I felt less of a need to control my parents or our relational
dance. Instead, I began to savor the infrequent but priceless
moments of connection, while continuing to grieve the loss
of felt intimacy—all the while trusting that She is right there
in the gray with us, guiding us all toward Love.

In the company of the Virgin-Warrior, we love by letting go.

10

god of white women

I opened my work email and was immediately assaulted by scores of messages from the Duke Divinity School faculty list serve.

"Oh, God." I cringed.

I hesitated before opening the first email because I knew only horror lay within. You see, a furious flurry of messages from the Duke Divinity faculty email list only meant one thing to me: another faculty race war. Though such race wars seemed as common as the Eucharist that was served at the weekly chapel services, I never grew accustomed to them. I winced at the sound of each "ping" alerting me to another message.

This time, the first message in the chain was from a white male colleague who invited us all to celebrate the publication of another white male colleague's most recent book, a novel. Okay, that's pretty typical. Duke Divinity is a prestigious school with lots of prolific scholars. People are constantly publishing books and patting each other on the back.

So far, so good.

The real trouble began when it became clear that the novel—again, authored by a white man—was on the topic of Black womanhood in America. Written in the first person, the novel told the story of one particular Black woman. This white male colleague had essentially colonized a Black woman's voice and story.

Bombs away.

The Black faculty responded with outrage. Well, the Black faculty with *tenure* responded with outrage. The rest of us sat on the sidelines wishing we could join the fight but were held back by the special flavor of white patriarchal terror that comes from needing your white colleagues to approve of you in order to keep your faculty position.

Obviously, no white man has any business assuming a Black woman's voice and telling her story. But my colleague's behavior was even more problematic because there's a long, violent history of Black women being silenced and forced into Mammy, Jezebel, Sapphire, and StrongBlackWoman identity prisons when other people have told their stories. As my Black tenured colleagues pointed out, it was unconscionable that a white man in the twenty-first century would follow in that tradition. Additionally, this particular white man wasn't even a social scientist or historian with an extensive background on race. (Not that these whitemale-god-starred "credentials" would have cleared him of wrongdoing.) No, he was a physician who, upon meeting a Black female patient and hearing her story of suffering, decided to share a version of it with the world. Apparently, the moral question of whether he, a white man, was authorized or qualified to share her Black female story didn't trouble him. Further, as another tenured Black colleague argued, Duke Divinity School has a number of scholars who *actually* study race and are *actually* Black who also often publish books. Yet our white male colleagues don't send out congratulatory all-faculty emails about our work. So, yeah, outrage. We were so tired of this nonsense.

Of course, the white male colleagues responded to the criticism with a mighty petulance that can only flow from whitemalegod's hallowed halls of academia. They accused the Black faculty of being too angry, of not affirming their white colleagues' "good intentions," and of being unintellectual.

As the shots continued, the Black faculty fired back with phrases from the ongoing Black Lives Matter movement. One Black female colleague ended her email with "Hands up, don't shoot." Another signed off with "I can't breathe."

It was getting personal. And it was also, finally, getting real.

You see, though these fiery race wars erupted often within the Duke Divinity faculty, they were always swiftly extinguished in a violently genteel, Southern Methodist sort of way. Even when we explicitly attempted to talk about race, the white colleagues shut the conversation down because they couldn't bear the discomfort. For example, that same year, a white male organizational consultant conducted focus groups among students, faculty, and staff, and determined that the school's racial climate was hostile. (No shit, Sherlock.) But when the consultant presented his data to the faculty and even shared verbatim quotes from his interviews, the predominantly white faculty refused to own up to its race problem.

One white female faculty member and alumnus shook her head and said, "This can't be right. These students don't really understand how to appreciate this school. I mean, I graduated from here not so long ago and I had a great experience! The students who participated in the assessment just seem really negative to me."

Another white female colleague and alumnus protested, "I don't even recognize the school that they're describing! I think their cynicism is clouding their judgment. In fact, I know a Black student who loves it here!"

A white male faculty member offered, "The data must be wrong. I've been a faculty member here for decades and this institution isn't perfect, but it sure has been good to me. I don't believe that it's been so terrible to these Black faculty and staff. There's no way."

A white male colleague said, "What do students know? They've only been here for a year or two. I've been here for much longer than that. I would know if this place was unwelcoming to Black people. It's not."

Another white male faculty member said, "I move to reject this report," as if a faculty vote to reject the report would make their anti-Blackness magically disappear.

Every single one of these white colleagues are the type of *Atlantic Magazine*–totin', NPR-listening, card-carrying liberals who "would've voted for Obama a third time" if they could've. Nevertheless, their discomfort with the truth trumped their supposed love for Black people. In other words, their white comfort was more important than Black pain. That sounds like white supremacy to me. The violently genteel, Southern Methodist sort of white supremacy.

You see, whitemalegod wants us to believe that he only exists in the Donald Trumps, the Robert E. Lee monuments, the word *nigger*, and in the institution of mass incarceration. As long as we can always point to some evil, anti-Black force *outside* of ourselves, we will never realize that we are complicit in whitemalegod's terror. As long as we think whitemalegod only exists *out there*, we will remain unaware of the ways in which he inhabits our emotions and behaviors. As long as we think that whitemalegod only exists in the most explicitly white supremacist and patriarchal spaces, we will never see that he is hiding in plain sight in institutions, spiritualities, neoliberalism, and, perhaps most covertly, in white women.

white femininity: whitemalegod's secret weapon

For the first several weeks of my walking pilgrimage, I debated whether to visit the famous Black Madonna of Orcival. It wasn't the walking distance that deterred me; She lived in a gorgeous Romanesque cathedral nestled in a charming medieval mountain town only fifteen miles away. Rather, I was hesitant to visit Her because I knew that, after a thousand years of being Black, She had undergone a mid-twentieth-century "renovation and restoration" process that whitened Her skin. I knew from photos that Her once gorgeous melanated skin was now a ghastly beige-ish pink. The incredible Black Madonna of Orcival now appears to be a white woman.

Nevertheless, in the end I decided to walk to Her because I wanted to see for myself what they had done to Her. Besides, as one of the most famous Black Madonnas in the world, I knew that since the 900s, thousands of socially oppressed pilgrims have walked along an ancient Roman road in order to pray to Her and find comfort in their distress. I wanted to walk that same Roman road in concert with the multitudes who had gone before me.

So, one crisp November morning, I set out for Orcival. The once mighty Roman thoroughfare is now simply a scenic trail that weaves and winds its way across a stunted volcanic mountain range. As I made my way along the forest floor covered in orange, red, and yellow leaves, I tried to imagine what the Black Madonna of Orcival had looked like before She was whitened. She must have been something special.

Though there are numerous Black Madonnas in the Auvergne region of France, few are as famous as the Black Madonna of Orcival. Even more so, though the Auvergne is known for its bounty of Black Madonnas, there are many, many more white Madonnas in the region. In fact, the white Madonnas are still the norm, even in a region that is known for its centuries-long devotion to the Black Madonna. Yet during the Middle Ages, the Black Madonna of Orcival—when Her skin was still Black—was one of the most visited

Madonnas in the region. There must have been something about Her that drew people to Her.

I mean, let's face it. In France, ancient Madonnas are a dime a dozen. It's easier to find a church that boasts an ancient Madonna statute than it is to find a Starbucks. So, there must have been something about Her that inspired pilgrims to journey on past the numerous other Black and white Madonnas in search of Her. For this reason, I longed to see Her original skin, yet I knew my longing would go unfulfilled. Her Black skin, the Black skin that had beckoned and nourished thousands of pilgrims, had been stolen from me. But I looked forward to examining Her facial features, Her posture, and Her expression. They may have stolen Her Black skin, but they can never steal Her Blackness.

After walking all morning, I finally approached the idyllic village of Orcival in the early afternoon. The entire village was closed for the tourist off-season, so I made my way straight to the stone cathedral. As I entered the church, I braced myself. I had heard that the Black Madonna of Orcival was the most heavily guarded Madonna of the region. But nothing could have prepared me for the spectacle I encountered. When I visited the Black Madonna of Mauriac, I had encountered a velvet rope blocking the altar and a sign forbidding anyone from crossing the rope. But this was something else. Instead of a rope and a flimsy sign, I saw a massive defense system surrounding the whitened Black Madonna of Orcival. A wooden barricade surrounded Her altar, a seemingly bullet-proof fortress encased Her body, and massive, blinding floodlights invaded every yard within throwing distance of Her.

She was more than heavily guarded; Her security system seemed on par with the most valuable crown jewels in the Tower of London. And there was no way I was getting near Her to gaze into Her eyes, mimic Her posture, and start to understand why so many pilgrims had been drawn to Her. Her fortress of defense, which kept me out, felt violent to my Black female body, which longed to draw near to Her.

Disappointed, I slumped in a pew and contemplated the fact that She, the whitewashed Black Madonna, was the most heavily guarded of all the Black Madonnas. She is even more heavily guarded than the Black Madonnas who have actually been stolen before. As I stared at Her from the enforced distance, I reflected on the fact that it is the whitened Black Madonna, not the most vulnerable Black Madonnas, who have been stolen, who is most heavily guarded.

I'll say that again: the whitened Black Madonna is more protected than the most vulnerable Black Madonnas. If that ain't that a metaphor for how white femininity is valued over Black femininity, I don't know what is.

As I sat in front of the whitewashed Black Madonna of Orcival, I began to make sense of what had happened to that race war at Duke Divinity. Let's see, we left off when it was finally getting real between the Black and white faculty.

That's right, my Black female colleagues had signed their protests with "Hands up, don't shoot" and "I can't breathe."

Not surprisingly, the petulant white men didn't like that. I mean, how dare we offend their delicate liberal, intellectual sensibilities by grouping them with racist cops and white nationalists? Couldn't we see that they're the "good guys"? It got ugly and eventually one white female colleague who calls herself a feminist entered the fray. But rather than speaking out on behalf of Black women, she essentially said, "Please remember that I'm battling a chronic illness. You all are my family. I need everyone to stop fighting and be nice to each other so that I can feel safe here." She was uncomfortable and she wasn't getting what she needed, so she shut down the conflict. But this wasn't just your garden-variety white defensiveness like the white faculty had displayed in response to the consultant's data. This white feminist weaponized her white femininity—using her individual, nonsystemic vulnerability to silence and delegitimize our Black femininity and systemic pain. Her tactic worked. Though they had persistently ignored the Black women's pain, all the white men immediately responded to the white women's pain and complied with her request to stop fighting. Consequently, the conflict that was just starting to get real abruptly ceased. In the end, whitemalegod continued to flourish at Duke Divinity School.

White femininity is one of whitemalegod's best disguises. Since the days of ol' Thomas Jefferson, white femininity has been an enemy of Black femininity and a way for whitemalegod to continue to exert his racial/gender hierarchy on the world. As Chanequa Walker-Barnes teaches us, white femininity has always been the "pure" femininity. As a result, it has always been more valuable and legitimate than "impure" Black femininity. For this reason, a white woman's "I'm uncomfortable" is always going to be valued over a Black woman's "I can't breathe." White patriarchy will always circle the wagons around white femininity, especially if it means it can continue to uphold the social pecking order by keeping Black women in their place at the bottom. As long as white women use their femininity to silence Black women's pain, whitemalegod lives on.

white feminism: whitemalegod's other secret weapon

Right after Donald Trump was elected, several Black LGBTQ Duke Divinity students and I traveled to Washington, DC, for the inaugural Women's March. All veteran justice demonstrators, we knew how to raise our collective voices, and we were energized and excited to participate in this historic march. Durham is about a five-hour drive from Washington, so we began our journey at dawn in order to make sure we got there before the march began. Hopped up on coffee and righteous indignation, we shared the ways in which a Trump presidency instilled terror in us as we traveled through the state of Virginia. After listening to my students tell their stories and share their reasons for participating in the Women's March, I shared my first reaction to the news that Trump had defeated Democratic presidential nominee Hillary Clinton.

When I woke up around 3:30 a.m. on the day after the election and saw the election results, my first thought went to the incarcerated students in my "Martin Luther King Jr. and Malcolm X" class at Central Prison, a maximum-security state penitentiary in Raleigh, North Carolina. Casualties of our (in)Justice Department, many of them were young Black men serving life sentences in whitemalegod's punitive reign of terror. My heart broke at the realization that their already hopeless situation just got worse. In the midst of my lament, I was already planning for action. I knew I couldn't stand by and watch the global injustice of a Trump presidency. I knew I had to keep fighting for justice even in the face of body-slamming pain and despair. That's why I was joining my students at the Women's March. I was marching for justice for my incarcerated Black students. My story simply echoed the stories of my students. All of us wanted to join in the fight for justice and equality for Black and LGBTQ people.

So, imagine our surprise when we arrived and encountered not a serious justice demonstration but a carnival full of white women wearing pink pussy hats. Clearly, these were bewildered white women who were shocked that their country—*their country*—hadn't protected them. Dealing with systemic disillusionment for the first time, these women did not know what it meant to engage in collective lament. These women did not know what it meant to protest, so they threw a party.

"This isn't a protest," one of the students said with dismay. "This is like a PRIDE parade."

It did have a PRIDE parade vibe. It had more of a celebratory and comradery vibe than a revolutionary edge. If we witnessed any anger, it was of the white feminist variety. Like, *You won't pay for my abortion!* As opposed to the Black feminist variety which is like, *STOP KILLING US!*

In an attempt to turn the parade into an actual march, our little group of six Black women decided to start a Black Lives Matter chant.

"Black Lives Matter! Black Lives Matter! Black Lives Matter! Black Lives Matter!" we called out in harmony.

Crickets.

Though we were intimately surrounded by tens of thousands of white women, no one joined us. Instead, the white women in pink pussy hats turned toward us and stared. The expression on their faces betrayed their utter confusion, "Don't they know that this has nothing to do with Black Lives Matter? Don't they understand that this is about Trump and how it's *not fair* that I voted against him and yet he is still president. Don't they know that this is about how it's just not fair?" We kept trying to get a Black Lives Matter chant going but no one ever joined in. Their white feminism could not accommodate our Blackness. Their white feminism excluded our Blackness.

Sociologist Jessie Daniels confirms, "To the extent that liberal feminism articulates a limited vision of gender equality without challenging racial inequality, then white feminism is not inconsistent with white supremacy. Without an explicit challenge to racism, white feminism is easily grafted onto white supremacy and useful for arguing for equality for white women within a white supremacist context."[1]

Dejected, we decided to head back to our rented van so we could begin the long journey back to Durham. As we made our way across the Washington Mall, we passed a similarly dejected Black woman slumped against a tree. A handmade cardboard sign proclaiming "white feminism is violence" leaned against her folded knee.

"Ain't that the truth," we affirmed as we nodded and

smiled at her. Indeed, white feminism is just whitemalegod in a pink pussy hat.

But as we left behind the pink-pussy-hat-adorned white-malegod of the Women's March and returned to Durham, we knew that we weren't actually escaping whitemalegod. We knew that whitemalegod is alive and well at Duke Divinity School in the ongoing silencing of Black female pain. We knew that whitemalegod is a shape-shifter who will become anything in order to maintain his systems of oppression.

god of white women

Like my white male colleague who, in his book, eagerly colonized the story and embodied the voice of a Black woman, whitemalegod can colonize any institution, person, idea, or culture. But many white women are so focused on the problem of patriarchy and how whitemalegod inhabits patriarchy that they can't see that whitemalegod inhabits white women too. The problem of whitemalegod isn't just that he's male, it's that he's white too. Just as all men have been conditioned by patriarchy, all white women have been conditioned by whiteness in both obvious and subtle ways. White women (and really, all who have been shaped by whiteness) must reckon with this ugly truth if they desire to truly commune with the Sacred Black Feminine.

For example, when white women hear the title of my book, the most common unsolicited response is an enthusiastic, "I know! I say that all the time: God is a woman and She is Black!"

I've received this response countless times, so I have a ready-made follow up: "So, tell me. How has this belief transformed your relationships to, solidarity with, and reparations toward Black women?"

Again, crickets.

Dumbfounded, they stutter, pause, and eventually sputter, "Well . . . I just believe it in my heart . . . Trust me, I really believe this . . . I even read a book about the Black Madonna!"

Ok, Karen, let's see here. You believe that God is a Black woman. In fact, you believe it so emphatically that you blurted your belief at a Black woman who is a complete stranger to you. And yet, as a white woman, you haven't considered what it would take for you to make such a proclamation with antiracist integrity?

And therein lies the problem. You see, it's relatively easy to see how my white male colleague's novel trespassed on the dignity and sacredness of Black women. It's easy to see the violent audacity in his assumption that he possessed the qualifications to author such a book. But it's harder to recognize the same pattern in the white women who, without hesitation or self-reflection, claim a belief in a God who does not look like them. For this too trespasses on the dignity and sacredness of Black women. Indeed, much like my white male colleague, these white women did not stop to ask if they were qualified either.

In fact, they had zero qualms about asserting their belief that God is a Black woman . . . to a complete stranger . . . who is obviously a Black woman . . . and has written a book called *God Is a Black Woman*. They did not pause to ask themselves, "What have I done to heal from my inherited white supremacist conditioning so that I am more likely to be a life-giving conversation partner for this sacred Black woman who was generous enough to share the title of her book with me?" And based on their inability to share how their belief has transformed their personal and systemic relationships with Black women, it's clear they didn't stop to ask themselves what a belief in the Sacred Black Feminine would *require* of them as white women. They did not stop to reflect on what it would take for them to make such a proclamation with integrity, with embodied practices that substantiated their belief.

You see, the actions of both my white male colleague and the white women I encountered are fueled by the same pillar of whiteness: *ontological expansiveness*. Race scholar and philosopher Shannon Sullivan defines ontological expansiveness as the way that white people "tend to act and think as if all spaces—whether geographical, psychical, linguistic, economic, spiritual, bodily, or otherwise—are or should be available for them to move in and out of as they wish."[2] I've nicknamed it *white sprawl* because, like suburban sprawl, it is driven by thoughtless expansion and extraction with very little concern for the well-being of the indigenous beings who inhabit the space.

White sprawl is the way in which white people are taught to claim and expand into any and all situations whether they have legitimately earned the right to be there or not. It's about audaciously believing that there is no spirituality that you cannot appropriate. It's about encountering an inspiring spiritual idea and automatically deciding it's yours for the taking. Further, white sprawl is about mastering your environment. It's about audaciously believing that there is no topic or area that you can't become an expert on. It's about believing you are qualified to write a book about the Black female experience because you have read some books on the topic and have had a few conversations with Black women. Additionally, it's about assuming that your presence or participation in a situation (like, a conversation with a Black woman) is an unequivocal good thing.

Like toxic masculinity is a form of patriarchal conditioning, white sprawl is a form of white supremacist conditioning. White sprawl fueled my white male colleague's audacity to write a novel about the Black female experience. And in the same way, white sprawl fueled the white women's proclamation that God is a Black Woman without asking whether they have done the work to make such an assertion with integrity. No matter its form, white sprawl is extractive and violent. Since it is socially conditioned, all white people (and all others who have been shaped by whiteness) naturally embody white sprawl unless they choose to actively work toward healing from their whiteness.

Indeed, unless white women who profess that God is a Black Woman disentangle themselves from the trappings of whiteness—such as white sprawl, white feminism, and the weaponization of white femininity—they will remain confined to *believe* in the Sacred Black Feminine and unable to move into the transformative *practice* of the Sacred Black Feminine, which involves active, consistent, strategic, embodied work toward the dismantling of the patriarchal *and* white supremacist systems. This is precisely how white-malegod continues to reign, even in white women who proclaim that God is a Black woman. For as long as the Sacred Black Feminine is just a belief, the white supremacist structure remains intact and whitemalegod remains the god of white women. Further, no matter our racial or gender identity, as long as the Sacred Black Feminine is just a belief, whitemalegod can even hide in the stories we tell about the Sacred Black Feminine—stealing Her voice, Her values, and Her solidarity with *all* Black women. Indeed, if we're not careful, whitemalegod can thrive undetected within our very idea of the Sacred Black Feminine.

Nevertheless, the Sacred Black Feminine welcomes us all with open arms. Unlike whitemalegod, She doesn't exclude anyone; Her circle is wide and all are welcome. But just because all are welcome doesn't mean all are ready. For though She is the Mother of all, She is especially the Mother of Black women. And though She is the protector of all, She is unapologetically Black and unapologetically concerned with the flourishing of Black women. Regardless of our racial identity, in order to experience the fullness of Her transformative love, we must get into formation around Her unapologetic Blackness. But we do not have to do this healing work on our own. She Who is Unapologetically Black empowers us all beyond mere beliefs and into transformative action. She is Love-in-Action and She is simply waiting for us to say YES.

11

She Who Is Unapologetically Black

They love our rhythm, but they don't love our Blues."

As I returned to Clermont-Ferrand after visiting the whitewashed Black Madonna of Orcival, I seethed with anger as this old quote sparred within me. Seeing the Black Madonna of Orcival's colonized, more "palatable" white body reminded me of all the ways that whitemalegod and his minions erase, silence, and cover over the full divinity, magic, and brilliance of Black women. Oh, they love having us around as long as we contort ourselves into the house nigger role that I inhabited so well. But when they can't control our magic, they put us back in our place. For example, they love having overqualified, supremely competent Black women in the thankless, supportive #2 role just below the mediocre white man who unjustly inhabits the top spot. But as soon as our uncontainable brilliance burns through their barely disguised mediocrity, they demote us. They love our voices when we sing about love (and not reparations). But as soon as we croon our pain, they confiscate our mic. They love us when we work like mules, never asking for more than barnyard slop. But as soon as we rise up with the knowledge that we are divine too and our influence begins to threaten theirs, they slap the *Jezebel* label on us and tell everyone that we are not to be trusted.

Whitemalegod's goal is to erase, silence, and cover over the full divinity, magic, and brilliance of Black women, just like he did to the whitewashed Black Madonna of Orcival. Even when people claim to believe that God is a Black woman, they struggle to actually embrace the full divinity of Black femininity. Oh, many people claim to love the *idea* of a Black female God. Indeed, the Black "Mammy" figure in pop culture has given our imaginations plenty of images of loving, doting, reliable, matronly, strong-but-soft Black women who are intimately present and safe in a way that whitemalegod can never be. But genuine devotion to and liberation by the Sacred Black Feminine also requires our embodied liberation from the white supremacy and patriarchy that rules our identities and behaviors. Liberation means going way beyond what is comfortable as we honestly examine the Sacred Black Feminine's *Blackness*.

Again, But Is She Black Tho'?

The whitened Black Madonna of Orcival, France, is proof that spiritual seekers are often unwilling to seriously engage Blackness. Just like She was whitewashed, our ideas about the

Sacred Black Feminine are often whitewashed so that She is more palatable and requires less of us. In other words, we want Her to be our Mammy, not a Black Feminist Revolutionary who annihilates every white supremacist and patriarchal fiber within us.

For example, when I talk about God as a Black woman, white people respond with, "Ohhh! Like *The Shack!*"

Actually, no. Not like *The Shack*. *The Shack* is whack.

The Shack is a mega-bestselling novel published in 2007 by a white man named William Paul Young. The story follows Mack, a pained white man who encounters God in the woods and is shocked to find that God is an ample, matronly Black woman named Papa, later played by Academy Award–winner Octavia Spencer in the major movie. When Mack asks why/how God is a Black woman, Papa essentially says, "You wouldn't have responded to me if I had been the old white man you expected me to be. You needed a different image of God with whom you could relate differently."

So, let me get this straight, Mack. God is Black and female because you need Her to be? How convenient.

God isn't just a Black woman when it conveniently suits the needs of white people. God is a Black woman. Period. Her identity does not revolve around what white men need. Nor does She exist to shock whites and men into some sort of spiritual experience. She's not here for white people's convenience. In fact, Her unapologetic Blackness is an inconvenience to white people who have long benefited from and participated in whitemalegod's oppression of Black people. Her unapologetic Blackness is the kind of inconvenience that forces people to reckon with a powerful Black woman who is nobody's #2 and nobody's Mammy. In fact, She is the kind of inconvenience that sets captives free because when Black women are no longer confined to the #2/Mammy boxes, everyone is free. Indeed, social science scholars agree that what's good for Black women is good for *all* people. The liberation of all Black women requires the dismantling of all systems of oppression—white supremacy, patriarchy, capitalism, Islamophobia, homophobia, transphobia, and more. These systems harm all of us. So, if Black women are thriving and free, it also means the oppressive systems have been eradicated and we are all thriving and free.[1]

But by centering his version of the Sacred Black Feminine around the needs and whims of white people, Young not only inhibits global liberation but he defaces Her, just like the midcentury renovators defaced the Black Madonna of Orcival. This is why I don't have any patience for *The Shack*. Whitemalegod is alive and well in *The Shack*; he's just disguised as a matronly Black woman named Papa.

But it's not just white men like Mack and *The Shack* author who violently contort the Sacred Black Feminine into something that suits them. For example, white women are some of the most fervent devotees of the Black Madonna and have written scores of books about Her. But they do not acknowledge that She is a Black woman who interacts with this world in an unapologetically Black female body. Rather, the focus is exclusively on Her female body as a clarion call for dismantling patriarchy. According to them, because She is female, we should fight for women's liberation. To be certain, it is not inherently harmful to recognize Her female body and be empowered by it. However, no attention is paid to Her Black body and there is no similar call for Black liberation. In fact, any discussion of Her Blackness is disembodied; She is a "dark force," a "blacklight" who shows us the way, a spirit-companion at the time of death. As a result, the Black Madonna is stripped of Her Blackness and all that it requires of us. Like the Black Madonna of Orcival, Her body is female but not Black, and seekers are never required to examine what it means to follow a God who is both female *and* Black. In this way, people who claim to love the Black Madonna can comfortably draw near to the idea of God as Black and female without dismantling the white supremacy that ravages their hearts and behaviors. In the end, whitemalegod lives on.

She's Not Petulant, but She Petty

As I pondered the triple travesty of the whitened Black Madonna of Orcival, the whitened Sacred Black Feminine in *The Shack*, and white women's whitened Black Madonna, my resentment boiled over.

"White people won't let us have anything, not even our Black Female God," I seethed.

Even though the trip to Orcival had been long and exhausting, I knew I needed to see an unapologetically Black Madonna before I returned home. So, as the sun set, I made a detour to the cathedral to visit Our Lady of the Good Death. Having visited Her countless times before, I knew She would see me and comfort my Black female pain.

As I walked along the cobblestone streets of Clermont-Ferrand's old city, I passed an antique bookshop that was perpetually closed. But this evening, a bright light illuminated the shop and the usually locked door was wide open. An aging French man sat behind the antique wooden desk that dominated the small and crowded shop. Since I had long wanted to check out this shop to see if there were any old books on the Black Madonna, I didn't dare waste this rare opportunity.

Peering into the shop, I noticed that everything about the bookseller and his shop were midcentury vintage—not because he was a hip vintage collector, but because he seemed to be living in a bygone era. I watched as he meticulously dipped an old-timey quill pen into a well of ink. Then I noticed that his gray wool pants, cashmere sweater, thin-rimmed spectacles, and steady but slow physical movements all whistled, "I'm from the '40s!"

I liked him immediately.

Upon entering, I greeted the bookseller with the customary "Bon soir!" and attempted to locate his religious books. But if any organizational system existed, it must have been hidden away in the bookseller's mind. As far as I could tell, the antique books, maps, and art were in glorious disarray.

Convinced I would never find what I was looking for on my own, I turned toward him, and in my extremely limited French asked if he had any books on the *Vierge Noire* (Black Virgin).

A gleam burst forth from his eyes as he energetically jumped up, dragged a heavy, wooden step stool over to the back corner of the shop, and vaulted himself up toward the top shelf. Triumphantly, he pulled down an old softcover book that had been wrapped in tissue paper in an attempt to preserve its fragile binding. As he handed me the book, he cautioned in French, *"Prudente!"* ("Careful!")

Oh, he didn't have to tell me that! There's nothing I'm more *prudente* about than the Black Madonna, but I made a show of gingerly accepting the book. As I opened to the title page, I saw that it was a 1936 French book that catalogued the Madonnas of the Auvergne region. The book held photos and descriptions of hundreds of obscure white and Black Madonnas, many of whom I had never encountered in my extensive research on the more famous ones. I casually flipped through the book looking for unfamiliar Black Madonnas and, within moments, my eyes landed on the fiercest Black Madonna I had ever seen.

"Whoa!" I thundered.

Don't get it twisted. All of the Black Madonnas exude fierce energy—whether it's their piercing eyes, their defiant stance, or their truth-telling titles. But this Black Madonna—called Our Lady of the Rock and dating to the 1100s—took fierce to a whole other level. One glimpse at Her and She'll have you saying, *"Prudente!"* too.

The book offered a faded, sepia-toned photo of Her statue in which the ebony-skinned Our Lady of the Rock stood firmly in a regal gown and hoisted a toddler-aged Black Baby Jesus on Her protruding hip. Her simultaneously exhausted and feisty posture telegraphed the "Not today colonizer, today is *not* the day!" vibe that Black women who have labored under whitemalegod's oppression often embody. But it was Her eyes that stole the show. Her face tilted downward and in the direction of Her hoisted hip, She was serving the most legendary side-eye I had ever seen. But Her side-eye wasn't directed at precious Black Baby Jesus. No, Her side-eye was directed at a white male priest kneeling at Her feet.

"Ohhh-Emmm-Geee," I said aloud.

The midcentury-but-not-hipster bookseller gave me a puzzled look.

"Wow. This white priest is actually a part of Her statue just so She can give him holy side-eye." I continued, mostly speaking to myself because the bookseller spoke little English.

Our Lady of the Rock, who I immediately began calling Our Lady of the Side-Eye, stole my heart and I promptly purchased the book. The photo of Her nine-hundred-year-old statue was exactly what I needed to remind me the Sacred Black Feminine refuses to be whitewashed and melted into the generic, anemic "divine feminine" pot.

Our Lady of the Side-Eye reminds us that She has been saying "Not today colonizer, today is *not* the day!" since the 1100s and She reminds us that She continues to echo Black women's cries.

Our Lady of the Side-Eye reminds us that She refuses to be misunderstood as anything other than definitely Pro-Black-Woman and anti-white-patriarchy.

Our Lady of the Side-Eye reminds us that the divine feminine alone will not liberate us from white patriarchy. She. Must. Be. BLACK.

Our Lady of the Side-Eye reminds us that, unlike white-malegod, She refuses to be petulant. However, Our Lady of the Side-Eye has no problem proclaiming that She is absolutely petty and will put a white man in Her statue just so She can tell the world how much She's not here for him.

#DoBetter

Our Lady of the Side-Eye's centuries-long existence makes clear to us that the Sacred Black Feminine will not tolerate whitemalegod's shenanigans—not in the form of cultural ideas, not in institutions, not in individuals, and not in our religious and spiritual spaces. But unlike whitemalegod, Her intolerance is not rooted in fearful petulance, nor is it powered by controlling shame. As the Virgin-Warrior teaches us, the Sacred Black Feminine has no interest in adopting whitemalegod's machiavellian monster tactics to whip us into shape. On the contrary, as a Black woman who cares deeply about the flourishing of *all* humans, She lends Her voice to a worldwide chorus of Black women singing an anthem titled "Do Better."

There's something magical and unique about the way that Black women are able to simultaneously express unconditional love for you while also calling you out. Those of us who are raised in whitemalegod's world have no concept of this mysterious concoction of love *and* high expectations. In whitemalegod's world, high expectations only exist in the absence of love, whereas love is understood to be a conflict-free, "everything goes" zone. In fact, research on the culture of whiteness reveals that white people have a difficult time dealing with conflict precisely because whiteness is designed to avoid conflict.[2] So, the beauty of someone lovingly but firmly calling you out is lost on many of us.

Indeed, since I grew up in a whitemalegod-worshipping Black family, I never associated high expectations with love. In fact, I still cringe when someone tells me "We need to talk" because, in my family, that phrase always meant that love would be conspicuously absent. In fact, my first experience of being called into the Sacred Black Feminine's loving accountability didn't occur until 2011, when I was trying to finish writing my first book. And by *trying*, I mean *failing*.

I was a mess. I had already missed two publication deadlines and I couldn't sit down to finish the damn book. Though I had successfully completed a PhD, whitemalegod's gaslighting taunts rang the loudest in my ears.

You're not good enough.

You're an imposter.

What wisdom could possibly come from a Black woman?

Wracked with insecurity—and years away from being connected to an unapologetically Black Female God who champions Black women's bodies, voices, and perspectives—I felt alone and scared. When I bravely shared my insecurity with my editor, he was supportive but had no meaningful advice for me. As a white man, he couldn't relate to the dehumanization I had endured throughout my life and how it silenced me now.

But one day, I took a risk and shared my insecurity with my beloved friend Cristin, one of the few Black women I knew back in those whitemalegod-saturated days. I barely had to finish my sentence before Cristin got into formation and gave me the most effective pep talk anyone has ever given me.

"You got this, Christena. You're the most brilliant person I know. Your work is crucial, and the world needs your book. You're the only person who can write this book, but don't worry, you're not alone. I'll be here every step of the way."

Then we made a plan for me to finish the book. And by *we*, I mean *Cristin* made a plan.

"Okay, you need to write a thousand words per day in order to meet your deadline. So, every day at 5 p.m., I'm going to text you to make sure you wrote your words. You better write them."

And so it went. Every morning, I woke up not wanting to write. But I'd envision the loving "do better" look on Cristin's face and know that, like clockwork, she would be texting me at 5 p.m. I knew that Cristin unconditionally loved me and would still be my friend if I didn't write. But I also knew Cristin would likely come over to my house and hover over my desk every single day if that's what it took for me finish the book. That's how much Cristin was invested in my best self. So, every day I wrote. I mean, what else was I going to do?

After ninety-two consecutive days of Cristin's texts, calls, affirmations, and loving accountability, I finished the book. In Cristin, I experienced the Sacred Black Feminine's transformative brew of Love-and-Expectations for the first time. And I could recognize the same brew in the statue of Our Lady of the Side-Eye.

In Her, the sparkling genius of Black Girl Magic, the nurturing wholeness of Black Mothering, and the fury of Black women's drive for excellence come together in a supremely loving insistence that we all do better. When we are truly transformed by Her, everything changes. Unlike whitemalegod who is all about head knowledge and the mastery of information, She requires full-bodied change. Since whitemalegod lives in the realm of the head, he wants us to stay there too. He wants us to consume books about the Sacred Black Feminine, talk about Her, and "know" things about Her because that will distract us from actually being transformed by Her. He knows She's been coming for him for centuries and he's desperate to prevent us from joining the hunt.

Indeed, in order to truly be healed by Her, we must join Her hunt. We must do better by coming into deeper alignment with Her "Not today colonizer" stance. No matter our race or gender, we have all been infected with whitemalegod's white patriarchy. Our knowing and unknowing participation in whitemalegod's reign of oppression is an assault on Her Black female body. So, we must search high and low for the internalized anti-Blackness and patriarchy we uphold in our minds, hearts, and bodies. We must decenter, protest, and dismantle cisgender white male power. We must center the wisdom, needs, and healing of the especially marginalized Black women like my little sister, Des. We must speak up in our whitemalegod-infested institutions even if we lose our jobs, friends, or standing. We must reform our white patriarchal family and generational patterns. We must create and sustain revolutionary matriarchal communities and organizations that center human needs over productivity and opt for transformative rather than punitive justice. And more than anything, we must eradicate the transphobia within ourselves and our communities. For if God is a Black woman, then She's a Black trans woman. Obviously.

The loving accountability of the Sacred Black Feminine asks everything of us. She asks that we surrender everything that whitemalegod has taught us to hold dear—not because She wants to control us, but because She wants to heal us.

She Is Black Because She Is Black

While visiting a Black Madonna in a church in Lucerna, Italy, scholar Leonard Moss asked the parish priest, "Father, why is the Madonna Black?"

The priest said, "My son, She is Black because She is Black."[3]

More than any other Black Madonna, Our Lady of the Side-Eye exudes unapologetic "I am Black because I am Black" Blackness. Though She lived miles away in a remote mountain chapel outside a tiny hamlet, I knew I had to visit Her.

I simply had to.

12

She Who Has the Final Word

Though I had already walked over three hundred and fifty miles across the Auvergne region of central France in order to commune with fifteen Black Madonnas, I knew that my journey to visit Our Lady of the Side-Eye would be my most epic yet. To be certain, some of my walking journeys had taken me into out-of-the-way villages. But between walking, ride shares, and the occasional train, I had always been able to return to my apartment in Clermont-Ferrand at night. But Our Lady of the Side-Eye lived in a sparsely populated area of the Auvergne that was more than a two-hour drive from Clermont-Ferrand. It wasn't until I looked for Her exact location on a map that I realized She doesn't even live in a village. In fact, compared to the hamlet in which She lives, the tiny villages I had encountered thus far were bustling, well-connected metropolitan cities. The hamlet of Mayres has about six homes, one church, and one chapel. That's it. No pub. No patisserie. No market. Just two churches and a few families. In the middle of nowhere.

"No wonder no one has ever heard of this jaw-dropping Black Madonna!" I mused.

Undeterred, I made a plan. First, I would take the train as far as I could to the town of Brassac-les-Mines. From there, I would embark on a three-day, forty-two-mile walking journey to visit Our Lady of the Side-Eye and two other Black Madonnas in the area. I was so excited I couldn't sleep the night before I left. Besides the thrill of visiting three ancient Sacred Black Feminine statues in an unexplored part of the Auvergne, I was excited to spend three straight days in my body and away from the bustle of the city.

She Who Never Fails

The first day was pure bliss. As soon as I stepped off the train, I was swallowed up by the expansiveness of this part of the Auvergne. For miles, all I could see were luscious hills and sky so blue it looked like an upside-down freshwater lake. As I began the six-mile walk to the first Black Madonna, who lived in the medieval village of Saint-Gervazy, I noticed how unpolluted and nonindustrial these country roads were. Though the roads were steadily trafficked, no thundering trucks kicked dirt in my face and no congested roundabouts befuddled me. It was just me, the meandering road, and the quiet buzzing of cars passing by.

Even though it is only a few miles from the train station, the village of Saint-Gervazy feels remote because it is nestled in the heart of horse country. As I walked by idyllic stables and through rolling fields of magnificent cows and goats, I was accompanied by a harmonizing chorus of whinnies, moos, and bleats. As I neared the village, the wooden fences turned to stone and the buildings became more frequent. Nevertheless, I hardly encountered any people. Though well-kept, it resembled a ghost town. Many of the homes were obviously unoccupied and there were almost no cars on the street. Puzzled, I stopped to chat with a woman named Hélène who was doing chores in a stable on the outskirts of town. In a mix of English and French, Hélène explained to me that this once-bustling village, like many others in the area, suffered from urban exodus. Since the 1960s, there'd been a steady pattern of kids growing up in the village, moving to Clermont-Ferrand for school or work, and never returning. Now, only about a few hundred aging people remain. Everyone else is scattered throughout France and beyond.

Within moments of chatting, Hélène asked me why I was in their little remote village. As soon as the words *Vierge Noire* left my mouth, joy erupted on her face. Unleashing a flurry of Frenglish, Hélène interrupted me.

Did I know that their Vierge Noire had been stolen and returned? Did I know that after being missing for seventeen years, She resurfaced at an art auction in Madrid? Did I know that, by then, She had exchanged hands five times and would need to be bought back? Did I know that the people of Saint-Gervazy fundraised and sold valuables and shared their inheritances so that, together, they could bring their Vierge Noire home? Did I know that people who had grown up in Saint-Gervazy and moved away years ago had returned in order to help bring their Vierge Noire home? Did I know that now the global children of Saint-Gervazy, who were once scattered by urbanism, are reunited by their collective love of their Vierge Noire? Did I know these things? Had I seen Her?

Hélène finally paused, swallowing about a gallon of fresh, country air. Her joyful reminiscing had produced droplets of tears that slowly rolled down her face and pooled at the end of her jaw.

With tears starting to sprout in the corners of my own eyes, I smiled at Hélène and in my own dialect of Frenglish told her that I had known about the theft and return, but not about the way that the community had gathered from near and far to collaborate on the Vierge Noire's homecoming. I told her I hadn't known that the Vierge Noire birthed a reunion among Saint-Gervazy's scattered family. I told her I hadn't known that the Vierge Noire's return enabled them all to return. I told Hélène that I too loved the Vierge Noire of Saint-Gervazy and had come all the way from the United States to see Her and to meet the people who loved Her. I told her that, in my own way, I too was returning home to Saint-Gervazy.

Hélène nodded and, with the abrupt matter-of-factness of a French woman who has spent her entire life running a country farm, said, "Then you are part of Saint-Gervazy too. You are one of us."

Returning to her chores, Hélène smiled at me and motioned toward the village church farther down the road. She didn't want to impede me any longer.

As I made my way to the Black Madonna, I knew I had already met Her—in Hélène and in the story of the people of Saint-Gervazy. But I still spent about an hour with Her in the empty church reflecting on how my own journey to see Her was, in fact, a coming home. For in the story of the Black Madonna of Saint-Gervazy, I recognized a deeper truth about the Sacred Black Feminine. Unlike whitemale-god, She can relate to our experiences of hopelessness because She too has been stolen. Even more, as a Black Mother, She knows the pain of stolen children too. She knows the pain of children stolen by mass incarceration, the war on drugs, systemic poverty, ableism, and other forms of violence. As someone who has endured the pain of personal loss and family loss, the Sacred Black Feminine empathizes with our pain and stands with us. When we are in the midst of loss and wondering if there is any hope, we can rest assured that She understands us and would never judge us for "lacking faith." And yet, just as the Black Madonna of Saint-Gervazy found Her way home, She also helps us find our way back home. The story of the Black Madonna of Saint-Gervazy answers the question "Where is God?" that I first asked years earlier as my beloved sister, Des, screamed for help in the midst of her psychotic pain. She is with us in the devastating loss and She also brings us back home—to Her, to hope, and to a community that will fight for us and embrace us just as we are. Though the Sacred Black Feminine is intimately acquainted with loss, She ultimately gets the last word.

I'm glad I needed to walk six more miles that day in order to reach my lodging for the night. I needed to be with these truths and allow them to sink in without rushing on to the next adventure. As the roots of truth deepened within me, the hours I spent walking across the countryside fertilized my embodied soul.

The Sacred Forest

The following morning, I rose early to begin the twenty-two-mile walk to the Black Madonna of La-Chapelle-Geneste. Still glowing from the previous day's spiritual riches, I started out with a rhythmic pep in my step that accompanied the soulful song in my heart. However, within a couple of miles of walking, I realized with horror that the bright green color that saturated the entire map I was using didn't indicate the bountiful presence of grassy fields as I had thought. Never one for geography, I was now beginning to realize that the color green on maps means mountains. As in, mountains you have to climb, like I was climbing right now, for *twenty-two miles*. Since both the Black Madonna of La-Chapelle-Geneste and Our Lady of the Side-Eye reside in mountain villages, it might have occurred to me that walking to them would require walking *up a mountain*. But it didn't.

Now, I shuddered as I realized that my idyllic walk through the French countryside was actually a serious back-packing trip. And as I walked farther and farther up, I realized I was entering a remote mountain wilderness. I wasn't just backpacking. I was *backcountry* backpacking. My cell phone reception was nonexistent. What looked like "roads" on the map were actually infrequently traveled, unkempt trails.

The wind began to howl and the temperature dropped as I reached higher elevations. And the route was so damn steep.

As I continued making my way up the mountain, I began to get low on water. Though I had brought four liters with me, I hadn't anticipated such strenuous hiking and hadn't brought a water filter along. With eight more miles to walk, I completely ran out of water. As I continued walking, I surveyed the landscape, searching for a home or working farm that didn't look completely deserted. I had never knocked on a door and asked for water before, but I was desperate to try anything. But I had no luck. The Haute-Loire area through which I was walking was an actual ghost town. Every once in a while, I would come upon a building, but it was always deserted. No cars, no people, nothing.

Approaching another steep incline, my throat was so dry that I began ferociously coughing. Stooped over, I coughed my way up the hill—and just when I thought I couldn't take another step—I saw a smokestack rising from an unknown source. My pace quickened! Smoke meant fire and fire meant people! As I neared the top of the hill, a big industrial building that boasted the words "St. Hilaire Distillery" appeared.

"A distillery? In the middle of nowhere?" I mused. "I sure as hell don't want vodka, but let's hope there's water.

As soon as I opened the door to the building, I was lovingly embraced by an intoxicating gust of lavender. As I entered, I discovered there was no vodka here. Much to my Sacred Black Feminine delight, this was an organic essential-oil distillery—a distillery run entirely by women and sourced by the surrounding flora and fauna. If my parched throat hadn't kept me grounded in reality, I would have thought I had died and gone to heaven.

The cheery woman at the front desk, Adele, took one concerned glance at me and asked if I needed water.

"Oui, oui," I nodded vigorously.

When she returned with a giant glass of *rosemary citrus–infused* water, I definitely thought I had died and gone to heaven. My desperate stop for water turned into an impromptu trip to the spa as Adele brought me some herbal salve for my aching knees and then invited me on a sensory tour of the distillery's industrial-sized vats of crushed herbs. Each stop on the tour was its own luxury aromatherapy session as we paused at each vat so I could learn about the particular herb within and then plunge my upper body into the vat and be enveloped by the exhilarating scent.

How incredible that I stumbled upon an essential-oil distillery years after I dreamt that the Sacred Black Feminine beckoned me into a magical forest full of blooming lavender! Though scared at the time, I followed Her call into the forest and into all of the freedom and healing within. Now, my surprise "spa day" in the middle of a French wilderness simply reminded me that following Her is so worth it. Truly, She Is Worth Seeking at All Costs.

As we made our way past the massive vats of cedarwood, black pepper, clove, eucalyptus, and numerous other herbs, each fragrance cloaked me in a different regal garment. Though my clothes remained muddy and sweaty, they were now infused with a luxurious aroma that lingered on my clothes and soul as I said goodbye to Adele and the other distillers and continued my journey.

Like peppermint essential oil invigorates the mind, my unexpected and lavish experience in the distillery awakened me to the possibility of other unexpected and lavish gifts on my journey. Though the journey remained cold and steep, I began to savor the glistening snow, relish the fresh pine, and allow the intricate animal tracks to pique my curiosity about forest life. By opening myself to the forest's wonder, I was reminded that the pre-Roman Gallic people who lived in this region thousands of years ago called this place the Sacred Forest. As I examined the winter fauna that bloomed despite the cold, the shimmering sunlight that courageously fought through the thick brush, and the haunting melody of the whistling wind, I couldn't help but agree that this forest is indeed sacred.

While I continued making my way through the Sacred Forest, I again recalled the forest in the dream I had at the beginning of my journey toward the Sacred Black Feminine. That forest hadn't seemed sacred to me. Back then, I was so terrorized by whitemalegod that I didn't know how to see that the lightless, unchartered forest could be sacred. I didn't know I could begin my uncertain journey with an eye peeled for wonder and an expectation of lavish surprises. But my journey toward the Sacred Black Feminine has taught me that the journey through the forest, while confusing and scary at times, is also full of the very luxurious wonder that I experienced in the distillery. When we are parched and most in need of reprieve, the Sacred Forest surprises us with lavish gifts.

In whitemalegod's world, we only get a "prize" if we somehow successfully survive his torturous obstacle course called life. But She's different. The Sacred Black Feminine's forest is sacred no matter where we are on our journey through it. It doesn't matter if we are taking our first shaky step into the forest. Our journey is sacred, and She offers us lavish gifts. It doesn't matter if we are midjourney and are bravely choosing to take another step forward after just having taken two steps back. Our journey is sacred, and She offers us lavish gifts. It doesn't matter if we have been steadily moving through the forest for a long time now. Our journey is sacred, and She offers us lavish gifts.

Unexpected, abundant, and healing gifts, like the ones I received at the essential-oil distillery in the midst of my journey, are littered throughout Her Sacred Forest. As we move into difficult and uncertain seasons on our journey toward wholeness, we can release the trepidation we've been conditioned to hold in our bodies and keep our eyes peeled for Her surprises.

The Mother of All Bling

Given the sumptuous offerings of the day, I shouldn't have been surprised that the Black Madonna of the village of La-Chappelle-Geneste is the most lavish, over-the-top, showing-out-and-showing-off Black Madonna I had ever seen. If I had to guess which Black Madonna Cardi B loves the most, I'd guess it's this one.

The Black Madonna of La-Chappelle-Geneste is so little known and lives in such a remote, unassuming mountain village that I hardly had any background information on Her. But I didn't need it; Her statue says *everything*. Actually, Her statue isn't a statue; it's a full-on Broadway production. Many of the Black Madonna shrines are about the size of a toddler, but the Black Madonna of La-Chappelle-Geneste's shrine is the size of a small home.

Four massive, Grecian columns and a series of ornate steps form an elaborate pergola around Her. Multitudes of clamoring (white) people surround the pergola, as if they are fawning over Her. (Because they are.) Nestled between the columns is an ostentatious gold arbor, and underneath the arbor sits the Black Madonna of La-Chappelle-Geneste in what is called the Wisdom Seat position. In other words, She is sitting upright, back erect, and feet planted firmly on the ground—as if She owns the place. (Because She does.) Both She and Her Black Baby are saturated from head to toe in glimmering clothing made of gold. In fact, the entire production is drenched in gold leaf. Large, gold stars form the backdrop, gold-lined clouds cover the fresco on the ceiling above, and gold accents dominate throughout. The only thing that *isn't* covered in gold is Her lips. They are adorned with bright red, sexy-time lipstick. Indeed, She is the Mother of All Bling.

But the best thing about the entire production is Her crown! Rather shockingly, an unassuming, plain gold crown sits on Her head. The simple crown seems out of place amidst the showy splendor and out of character for the Mother of All Bling. However, four well-fed-looking (white) babies hover in the air just above the Black Madonna of La-Chappelle-

Geneste, hoisting a ginormous gold crown above Her head. Her *real* crown is so big and luxurious that it would dwarf Her if She wore it, so little white babies carry it for Her. Her Holy Bling is literally so massive that it would be a pain to carry it, so Her reparations entourage carries it for Her. Free of the StrongBlackWoman chains, the Mother of All Bling isn't going to wear Her holy self out. She's gonna get that rest, and She's gonna look good while doing it. She's the Treat Yo' Self Madonna.

As I sat before Her, taking in the divine spectacle of Her splendor, it began to make sense to me that She is the Black Madonna who holds court over the Sacred Forest through which I had just walked. She is the source of the sacred lavishness, rest, bougieness, sensuality, and reparations that we are promised on our journey. In the midst of my forty-two-mile journey to Our Lady of the Side-Eye, I encountered the Mother of All Bling in an essential-oil distillery, in a Sacred Forest, and in a remote, unassuming mountain village. She's everywhere, just waiting to shower Her bling on us. She obviously doesn't hold out on Herself, so She obviously won't hold out on us.

Our Lady of the Side-Eye

I awoke early the following morning, eager to walk to Mayres to meet Our Lady of the Rock, who I called Our Lady of the Side-Eye. I couldn't wait to come face to face with the truth-telling, can't-stop-won't-stop, *not-today-colonizer* boldness that shoots from Her eyes, stance, and every limb. Not surprisingly, the Mother of All Bling lives only a breezy four miles from Our Lady of the Side-Eye. As I hiked through the Sacred Forest, I imagined the two Sacred Black Women sharing their brazen energy, egging each other on through the centuries. The forest felt ripe with liberating energy as I walked among trees that had lived in the company of these two Women for centuries.

Though my legs were exhausted from over forty miles of mostly uphill journeying, my pace quickened as I neared Mayres. As I rounded a forest bend, I spotted Our Lady of the Side-Eye's lonely chapel high up on an upcoming hill. Energized, I started to jog, and my heavy pack jounced awkwardly on my back. I lumbered across a rickety wooden backcountry bridge and up the hill. But as soon as I started the ascent, I realized it was so steep that I needed to use my hands to scramble up the hill. Frustrated by this minor impediment, I threw off my backpack and left it at the base of the hill so I could scramble faster. As I neared the top of the hill, the slope decreased and I was able to break into a swift gallop. The little mountain chapel was just a few yards away!

But when I arrived, the door was locked and the lights were off. Exhausted and out of breath but desperate to see Her, I returned to the foot of the hill to grab my backpack and then frantically ran to the nearby village, banging on every door and shouting for help in my Frenglish. After speaking with several villagers, I learned that the chapel is only open once a year, on September 8, which is Her feast day. My heart sank at this anticlimactic news. I had walked forty-two miles and I wouldn't get to see Her.

A kind man showed me to the village church, where a gorgeous picture of Her shimmered in the stained-glass window above the altar. As I sat there taking time to gingerly and lovingly hold space for my colossal disappointment, it occurred to me that, yes, it would have been amazing to meet Her face-to-face. But the fact that I walked forty-two miles across a winter mountain range in order to meet Her is pretty solid proof that Our Lady of the Side-Eye has been beside me and within me all along.

Our Lady of the Side-Eye has been beside me and within me as I tentatively took my first step into the unknown forest. Our Lady of the Side-Eye has been beside me and within me as I said goodbye to spiritual communities and relationships that were harming me. Our Lady of the Side-Eye has been beside me and within me as I escaped the Christian plantation. Our Lady of the Side-Eye has been beside me and within me as I have bravely uncovered the ghastly wounds of my past. Our Lady of the Side-Eye has been beside me and within me as I have "made a way out of no way" toward a spirituality that honors and affirms my experience as a Black woman. Our Lady of the Side-Eye has been beside me and within me as I walked four hundred miles across central France in search of ancient images of the Sacred Black Feminine. Our Lady of the Side-Eye has been beside me and within me all along.

As I returned to Clermont-Ferrand, I treasured the truth that Our Lady of the Side-Eye is beside me and within me. For I knew that many other challenges would arise as I continued my journey toward liberation. I knew I could no longer work at the Duke University plantation if I wanted to be free of whitemalegod's capitalistic snares. I had an inkling that the Black Madonna was simply a portal into the ageless Sacred Black Feminine that exists outside of Christianity. I knew that my journey toward the Sacred Black Feminine would require that I bravely seek out the very deities Christianity has vilified—like Isis of ancient Egypt, Kali of Hinduism, Black Artemis of ancient Ephesus, and Yemoja of Yoruba. Even more, I was beginning to suspect that my continued liberation would involve the end of many more unhealthy relationships so that life-giving ones could be born. As I finished my four-hundred-mile walking pilgrimage, I knew my journey had actually just begun. But I was certain that Our Lady of the Side-Eye was beside me and within me as I took the next uncertain steps.

Home

I would be remiss if I left you with the impression that my time in France was consumed with the Black Madonnas. In truth, I spent a copious amount of time shopping for vintage clothes and items. You see, like the Mother of All Bling, I love lavish, over-the-top beauty. And the French flea markets and vintage shops are legendary for their splendid offerings. When I wasn't walking to a Black Madonna, I scoured the Auvergne markets for vintage apparel and trinkets. During my five weeks in France, I unearthed plenty of fabulous vintage clothing, for instance, a dramatic 1985 Thierry Mugler couture jumpsuit that was simply *made* for me. To be sure, I also kept my eyes peeled for a small Black Madonna statue to bring home with me. But since I hadn't encountered any, I figured I wasn't meant to find one on this trip.

On my final evening in France, I decided to take one last walk in Clermont-Ferrand's old city. Wandering down a winding, cobblestone street I had never explored before, I stumbled upon an antique shop with huge, squeaky-clean windows just beckoning me to peer inside. My curiosity got the best of me and, as I looked beyond the window display, I discovered a mystical, dark wooden Black Madonna staring back at me.

I entered the shop and learned that this seventeenth-century solid-pearwood Black Madonna came from a church in a tiny village in the Burgundy region of France. Not in museum-quality shape (and, thus, affordable to me), She looked well loved. It was obvious that real people had loved Her, touched Her, and prayed to Her throughout Her four-hundred-year lifetime. I knew She was for me, so I purchased Her and carried Her three-year-old-child-sized body back to my apartment.

It wasn't until I got home that I began to worry about how I would get Her back to the United States. At about two and a half feet tall, She was too big to put in my carry-on bag. And there was no way I was putting a pricey, fragile antique in my checked luggage. Out of ideas, I knew exactly who I could count on to help me get my cherished Black

Madonna home: Dad. The most experienced international traveler I have ever encountered, Dad knows all the travel hacks. Whenever I need advice on anything travel related—from which hotel chain has the best rewards program, to the best luxury spa in Bali, to the most exquisite Northern Italian cuisine in Boston's Back Bay, to the most spacious airport lounge at London's Heathrow—I always turn to Dad. He's like Trip Advisor but make it bougie and Black.

As I dialed Dad, I savored the fact that, though our relationship had changed, a loving connection remained. I knew that even though he didn't quite understand my devotion to the Black Madonna, he would do everything he could to get my Black Madonna safely home.

When I shared my dilemma with Dad, he responded with the "Oooooo ooooo ooooo" that often erupts from his mouth when he's excited about an idea. Dad and I share an adventurous spirit, so it's no surprise he was invigorated by the possibility of concocting a plan to get a forty-pound, thirty-inch-tall Black Madonna through security, past the boarding gate, and beyond US customs.

Dad's plan was pure genius: wrap Her in a blanket and then again in your winter coat and carry Her over your shoulder like you would carry a sleeping toddler.

I loved the plan. Nevertheless, I tossed and turned as the night wore on, my fears sprinting laps around the interior of my head. What if I am stopped at the boarding gate and the gate agents discover my ruse and I am forced to put Her in my checked luggage? What if She gets destroyed by the baggage handlers? What if I don't make it through US customs and She is detained? What if I'm charged an exorbitant amount of import taxes and I can't afford to keep Her?

But when I reminded myself of the Black Madonna of Saint-Gervazy who found Her way home, I began to breathe more deeply, and my fears receded. *She can take care of Herself,* I offered myself as a lullaby. *If She's meant to come home, She will find a way,* I cooed to myself. Within moments, I fell asleep within Her trustworthiness.

The following day, when I boarded my first flight in Clermont-Ferrand and then my second and final flight in Paris, I did exactly what Dad suggested and pretended She was a sleeping child and that I was Her mother. I even rocked Her as I waited to board, for dramatic effect. The only time people raised their eyebrows at me was when I put Her in the overhead compartment.

As my plane landed in the United States, I knew we just had to get through the customs entry checkpoint and then we'd be home free. During the long deboarding process, my arms grew tired from holding Her forty-pound body. Nevertheless, I didn't put Her down. I couldn't abandon the ruse, not when we were this close. After we finally deplaned and began the long walk down the corridor to the customs entry point, my nerves spiked. We were so close, but I was afraid we wouldn't make it!

However, when I approached the customs official, he didn't see my nerve-wracked face. Instead, he saw a jet-lagged young mother struggling to carry a heavy, sleeping child.

Ushering me forward, the customs official didn't bother to inspect my passport or ask me to declare any imported goods. He just lovingly nodded at my "sleeping child," smiled at me, and said, "Welcome home, Mama."

"Yes. Welcome home, Mama." I whispered to Her.

We were home.

acknowledgments

The journey home is a village-wide effort—and my village is global, interfaith, and fierce. My decade-long healing transformation, five-week walking pilgrimage, and multiyear effort to bring this book to life are the fruit of many loving conversations, countless hours of spiritual and therapeutic practices, dramatic revisions, equally dramatic sob sessions, heaps of practical guidance, and explosive laughter.

To the villagers who helped birth this book: profuse gratitude to my agent Chris Park, whose strategic wisdom, intersectional advocacy, feisty humor, and mysticism accompanied each step toward publication. Thank you to everyone at HarperCollins/HarperOne who brought enthusiasm and prowess to this book: Judith Curr, Adrian Morgan, Lisa Zuniga, Joan Keyes, and Andrew Jacobs. A special thank you to my lead editor, Katy Hamilton, and an incredible editorial team: Chantal Tom, Tracy Sherrod, Anna Paustenbach, and

Alexa Allen. You all passed the baton as elegantly as an Olympic relay squad and I'm grateful for each of your unique contributions. Thank you to Golden Collier, Marlena Willis, and Cinelle Barnes for your editorial guidance on early versions of the manuscript. Thank you to Delita Martin for graciously allowing us to use your grounded-yet-otherworldly art on the cover. I couldn't have hoped for a more inviting and stimulating image of the Sacred Black Feminine. Thank you to my assistant, Lisa Heaner, for zealously patrolling my margins as I poured my entire being into this book. Thank you to my beloved Patreon community for supporting me financially and sending me hundreds (!!) of encouraging postcards while I finished the final chapters. Y'all give me so much life! Merci beaucoup to the Sisters of St. Clare in Chamalières, France—especially Sisters Paule and Hanna—for lovingly hosting me at the monastery for four weeks in 2019 while I wrote the pages that became chapters 1 and 3.

To the villagers who practically supported my walking pilgrimage: thank you to Mardi Fuller, Lori Herold, and Jonathon Stalls for sharing pragmatic wisdom as I prepped for such a physically demanding adventure. Thank you to Jim Dahlin for braving wind, rain, and elevation gain while walking with me to the Black Madonna of Orcival. Thank you to Victor Greene for schlepping from Paris to Clermont-Ferrand in order to gift me with your presence. Thank you to three strangers, Noel of Braval-sur-Doulon, Jean of Orcival, and Ines of Thuret, for generously spending hours helping me find my way back to my lodging.

To the villagers who cojourneyed as healers, teachers,

and companions: Julia Kaplinska, Amy Elliott, Judith Lies, Annie Goglia, Susan Main, Kelsey Blackwell, Kira Allen, Coke Tani, Toni McClendon, Lourdes Bernard, Sasha Cohen, Sonja B., Stacy Boorn, Andrea B., Phileena Heuertz, Valerie Cooper, Rebecca Kuhns, Ed Wimberly, Mirabai Starr, and Pixie Lighthorse. My heart is full of love and gratitude for each of you.

To my beloveds: Cristin, Mardi, Zakiya, Marlena, and SK. Each of you sprinkles different flavors of wisdom, joy, and strength on my journey. Thank you for being you and for sticking with me as I bushwhacked into the thicket.

To my brother John: thank you for creatively and earnestly loving me as our spiritual paths diverged.

To my sister Des: you are all the evidence I need that God is indeed a Black woman. I delight in you, and I'm so thankful that you're my sister.

To the Radiant Darkness that exists in all beings, especially Black women: Thank you for setting me free and leading me home.

notes

1

1 Kenny Moore, "Sportsman of the Year: The Eternal Example," *Sports Illustrated*, December 21, 1992, 21.

2 Hazel Rose Markus and Alana Conner, *Clash! 8 Cultural Conflicts that Make Us Who We Are* (New York: Hudson Street Press, 2013).

3 Clarissa Pinkola Estés, *Untie the Strong Woman: Blessed Mother's Immaculate Love for the Wild Soul* (Boulder, CO: Sounds True, 2011).

4 Pinkola Estés, *Untie the Strong Woman*.

2

1 Andrew Harvey, *The Return of the Mother* (Berkeley, CA: Frog, 1995); Matthew Fox, *The Hidden Spirituality of Men: Ten Metaphors to Awaken the Sacred Masculine* (Novato, CA: New World Library, 2008); Marija Gimbutas, *The Living Goddesses* (Berkeley: Univ. of California Press, 1999); Merlin Stone, *When God Was a Woman* (New York: Harcourt Brace Jovanovich, 1978).

2   Harvey, *Return of the Mother*, 180.

3   Matthew Fox, *The Hidden Spirituality of Men: Ten Metaphors to Awaken the Sacred Masculine* (Novato, CA: New World Library, 2008), 8.

4   Jacquetta Hawkes, *Dawn of the Gods* (London: Chatto and Windus, 1958).

5   Merlin Stone, *When God Was a Woman* (New York: Harcourt Brace Jovanovich, 1978), 67.

6   Stone, *When God Was a Woman*, 103–25.

7   Fox, *Hidden Spirituality of Men*, 7.

8   Fox, 10.

9   Harvey, *Return of the Mother*, 180.

10   Julian of Norwich, *Revelations of Divine Love* (Exeter: Univ. of Exeter, 1976).

11   Marguerite of Oingt as cited in Harvey, *Return of the Mother*, 388.

12   St. Bernard de Clairvaux as cited in Harvey, *Return of the Mother*, 385.

13   Pope John Paul I as cited in Leonardo Boff, *The Maternal Face of God: The Feminine and Its Religious Expressions* (San Francisco: Harper & Row, 1987).

14   Ivy Helman, "On Snakes," *Feminism and Religion*, February 11, 2018.

15   Sven Kachel, Melanie C. Steffens, and Claudia Niedlich, "Traditional Masculinity and Femininity: Validation of a New Scale Assessing Gender Roles," *Frontiers in Psychology* 7 (July 5, 2016), https://www.frontiersin.org/article/10.3389/fpsyg.2016.00956.

16   Fox, 35.

17   "Whiteness," National Museum of African American History & Culture, accessed May 25, 2021, https://nmaahc.si.edu/learn/talking-about-race/topics/whiteness.

18 Curtiss Paul DeYoung, *Coming Together in the 21st Century* (Valley Forge, PA: Judson Press, 2009).

19 Edward J. Blum and Paul Harvey, *The Color of Christ: The Son of God and the Saga of Race in America* (Chapel Hill: Univ. of North Carolina Press, 2012).

20 Kelly Brown Douglas, *The Black Christ* (Maryknoll, NY: Oribs Books, 2019), 12.

21 Samuel B. How, *Slaveholding Not Sinful: Slavery, the Punishment of Man's Sin, Its Remedy, the Gospel of Christ* (New Brunswick, NJ: Terhunes Press, 1856, reprinted, Freeport, NY: Books for Libraries Press, 1971).

22 Frederick Douglass, "Slaveholding Religion and the Christianity of Christ," in *Afro-American Religious History*, ed. Milton C. Sernett (Durham, NC: Duke Univ. Press), 101.

23 David Pilgrim, "The Jezebel Stereotype," updated July 2012, https://www.ferris.edu/jimcrow/jezebel/.

24 Melissa V. Harris-Perry, *Sister Citizen* (New Haven, CT: Yale Univ. Press), 56.

25 Chanequa Walker-Barnes, *Too Heavy a Yoke: Black Women and the Burden of Strength* (Eugene, OR: Cascade Books), 84.

26 Moya Bailey, *Misogynoir Transformed: Black Women's Digital Resistance* (New York: NYU Press, 2021).

27 Richard Rohr, *Eager to Love: The Alternative Way of Francis of Assisi* (Cincinnati, OH: Franciscan Media, 2014), 211–13.

28 James A. Borland, *Christ in the Old Testament: Old Testament Appearances of Christ in Human Form.* 2nd ed. (Chicago: Moody, 1978).

29 Kelly Brown Douglas, "Is Christ a Black Woman? A Womanist Understanding of Christ Is Rooted in Healing Fractured Communities," *The Other Side* 30 (1994): 11.

30   Clarissa Pinkola Estés, *Untie the Strong Woman: Blessed Moth-er's Immaculate Love for the Wild Soul* (Boulder, CO: Sounds True, 2011), 34.

3

1   Clarissa Pinkola Estés, *Untie the Strong Woman: Blessed Moth-er's Immaculate Love for the Wild Soul* (Boulder, CO: Sounds True, 2011),145.

2   Actual quote: Womanism "takes seriously black women's experiences as human beings who are made in the image of God; it affirms and critiques the positive and negative attri-butes of the church, the African American community, and the larger society." In Linda E. Thomas, ed., *Living Stones in the Household of God: The Legacy and Future of Black Theology* (Minneapolis, MN: Fortress Press, 2004).

3   Jacquelyn Grant, *White Women's Christ and Black Woman's Jesus* (Atlanta, GA: Scholars Press, 1989).

4   Monica Coleman, *Making a Way Out of No Way* (Minneapo-lis, MN: Fortress Press, 2008).

5   *Greater Good Magazine*, "What Is Mindfulness?" May 26, 2021, https://greatergood.berkeley.edu/topic/mindfulness /definition.

6   Pinkola Estés, *Untie the Strong Woman*, 146.

7   Frederic Chapman, ed., *The Works of Anatole France in an English Translation* (New York: John Lane, 1909). https://play .google.com/store/books/details?id=quYMAQAAIAAJ &rdid=book-quYMAQAAIAAJ&rdot=1.

8   Charles Horton Cooley, *Human Nature and the Social Order* (New York: Charles Scribner's Sons, 1902).

9   National Park Services, "North Star to Freedom," https:// www.nps.gov/articles/drinkinggourd.htm.

10   PBS.org, "Harriet Tubman," https://www.pbs.org/wgbh /aia/part4/4p1535.html.

4

1   Natasha Marin, *Black Imagination* (San Francisco, McSweeney's), 11.

2   Marin, *Black Imagination*, 46.

3   Marin, 35.

4   Marin, 37.

5   Marin, 32.

6   Marin, 34.

7   Marin, 71.

8   Shamus Khan, *Privilege: The Making of an Adolescent Elite at St. Paul's School* (Princeton, NJ: Princeton Univ. Press, 2021), 5.

9   National Women's Law Center, "Stopping School Pushout for: Girls of Color," https://nwlc.org/resources/stopping-school-pushout-for-girls-of-color/; Lauren Camera, "Black Girls Are Twice as Likely to Be Suspended in Every State," *US News & World Report*, https://www.usnews.com/news/education-news/articles/2017-05-09/black-girls-are-twice-as-likely-to-be-suspended-in-every-state.

10 Thomas Jefferson, *Notes on the State of Virginia*, 1781, https://www.google.com/books/edition/Notes_on_the_State_of_Virginia/NgKidsPa_QoC?hl=en&gbpv=0.

5

1   Ntozake Shange, "we need a god who bleeds now," *A Daughter's Geography* (New York: St. Martin's, 1983), 61.

2   Andrew Harvey, *The Return of the Mother* (Berkeley, CA: Frog, 1995), 359.

3   Clarissa Pinkola Estés, *Untie the Strong Woman: Blessed Mother's Immaculate Love for the Wild Soul* (Boulder, CO: Sounds True, 2011), 70.

4   Heide Göttner-Abendroth, "Matriarchies Are Not Just a
    Reversal of Patriarchies," *Feminism and Religion*, February 16,
    2020, https://feminismandreligion.com/2020/02/16
    /matriarchies-are-not-just-a-reversal-of-patriarchies-a
    -structural-analysis-by-heide-goettner-abendroth/.

5   Bella DePaulo, *Singled Out: How Singles Are Stereotyped,
    Stigmatized, and Ignored, and Still Live Happily Ever After*
    (New York: St. Martin's Press, 2006).

6   Ezekiel 16:6.

6

1   Nayyireh Waheed, *Salt* (CreateSpace, 2013), 6.

2   Andrea E. Shaw, *The Embodiment of Disobedience: Fat Black
    Women's Unruly Political Bodies* (Lanham, MD: Lexington
    Books, 2006), 3.

3   Sabrina Strings. *Fearing the Black Body: The Racial Origins of
    Fat Phobia* (New York: New York Univ. Press, 2019), 17.

4   Strings, *Fearing the Black Body*, 17.

5   Strings, 42.

6   Shaw, *The Embodiment of Disobedience*, 12.

7   Chanequa Walker-Barnes, *Too Heavy a Yoke: Black Women and
    the Burden of Strength* (Eugene, OR: Cascade Books), 95–96.

8   J. H. Langlois, L. Kalakanis, A. J. Rubenstein, A. Larson,
    M. Hallam, and M. Smoot, "Maxims or Myths of Beauty?
    A Meta-Analytic and Theoretical Review," *Psychological Bul-
    letin* 126, no. 3 (May 2000): 390–423.

7

1   Brandt Williams, Curtis Gilbert, and MPR New Staff,
    "#BlackLivesMatter Protest Fills Mall of America Rotunda,"
    MPR News, December 20, 2014, https://www.mprnews
    .org/story/2014/12/20/moa-blacklivesmatter-protest.

2   J. Mase III and Lady Dane Figueroa Edidi, eds., *Black Trans Prayer Book* (Lulu.com), 74.

8

1   Methods of Controlling Slaves, *Digital History*, https://www.digitalhistory.uh.edu/teachers/lesson_plans/pdfs/unit4_5.pdf.

2   Chanequa Walker-Barnes, *Too Heavy a Yoke: Black Women and the Burden of Strength* (Eugene, OR: Cascade Books), 96.

3   Sue Monk Kidd, *The Dance of the Dissident Daughter* (San Francisco: HarperSanFrancisco, 1996).

4   Curtis Yee, "Cru Divided over Emphasis on Race," *Christianity Today*, June 3, 2021, https://www.christianitytoday.com/news/2021/june/cru-divided-over-emphasis-on-race.html.

9

1   John Bunyan, *Pilgrim's Progress* (Abbotsford, WI: Aneko Press, 2014), 5.

2   Tina Shermer Sellers, "How the Purity Movement Causes Symptoms of Sexual Abuse," updated September 1, 2020, https://www.tinaschermersellers.com/post/how-the-purity-movement-causes-symptoms-of-sexual-abuse.

3   Clarissa Pinkola Estés, *Untie the Strong Woman: Blessed Mother's Immaculate Love for the Wild Soul* (Boulder, CO: Sounds True, 2011).

4   Andrew Harvey, *The Return of the Mother* (Berkeley, CA: Frog, 1995).

5   J. Mase III and Lady Dane Figueroa Edidi, eds., *Black Trans Prayer Book* (Lulu.com, 2020), 74–75.